Book of Black Heroes

Volume Two

Great WOMEN In The Struggle

AN INTRODUCTION FOR YOUNG READERS

Toyomi Igus
Editor

Toyomi Igus, Veronica Freeman Ellis, Diane Patrick, Valerie Wilson Wesley
Contributing Writers

8 7 6 5 4

FOREWORD

Within these pages you will find stories about some of the world's most amazing women. While most have lived in different periods of history and were faced with different kinds of obstacles, they all share a common heritage and a common goal: to improve the lives of their people.

Most of these stories are not pretty ones. These women's lives have not been idyllic, so you'll find no fairy tales here. Yet each in its own way is a success story, a heroic story that resulted from facing difficulties, testing limits, coping with disappointments, and finding strength in the struggle.

While we have tried whenever possible to explain honestly why events took place, children who read this book will no doubt ask their parents and teachers some hard-to-answer questions. And so they should. If *Great Women in the Struggle*'s only achievement is to stimulate meaningful dialogue and interaction between youngsters and their teachers, then we have accomplished our primary goal.

We recognize that many deserving women have not been profiled on these pages and we welcome your comments and suggestions for the next *Book of Black Heroes*. Our hope is that parents and educators will use this volume as a guide for further discussion of the larger issues (a suggested reading list is printed in the back). We also hope that children of all races and both genders will be encouraged to read this book, for these stories are not merely about black women for black children. They are stories about the power and resilience of the human spirit, which is characteristic of all people.

Enjoy *Great Women in the Struggle*. We know that those who read this book will take heart and be enlightened by it—just as we were.

CONTENTS

I AM A BLACK WOMAN

I
am a black woman
tall as a cypress
strong
beyond all definition still
defying place
and time
and circumstance
    assailed
       impervious
          indestructible
Look
    on me and be
renewed

—from "I Am a Black Woman,"
          Mari Evans

Freedom Fighters

BREAKING DOWN BARRIERS

Two elderly women attend a 1900 convention of former slaves.

Ain't I a woman?
I have ploughed and planted
and gathered into barns,
and no man could head me!
And ain't I a woman?
. . . If the first woman God ever made
was strong enough
to turn the world upside down
all alone,
these women together ought to be able
to turn it back,
and get it right side up again!

—Sojourner Truth

Nzingha

**Queen-Warrior
1582–1663
Birthplace: Angola, Africa**

A cunning and prudent virago . . . so generously valiant that she never hurt a Portuguese after quarter was given and commanded all her servants and soldiers alike.

—description of Queen Nzingha by a Portuguese commanding officer, 1646

When Nzingha was growing up, the Portuguese were trying to invade her country and take her people as slaves. She was a member of the Jaga people who lived in an area of Africa called Ndongo, now known as Angola. Nzingha's brother, Ngola, the king of Ndongo, fought off the Portuguese invasion for many years, but it wasn't until he died and Nzingha became queen that the Portuguese faced their most cunning rival. Nzingha became famous for her bravery, intelligence, and determination to keep her people free.

During her brother's reign, Nzingha was sent to represent him at a peace conference with a Portuguese governor. When the governor refused to give Nzingha a chair, she defied him and his lack of manners by sitting on the back of one of her attendants. Nzingha proved to be a brilliant negotiator, successfully developing a treaty that would best benefit her country.

Nzingha was also an ambitious woman. Some historians have reported that she poisoned her own brother to take his throne. Others believe that the story was made up to discredit her. Whether or not the story was true, Nzingha proved her worthiness as a fearless leader. Her first official act as queen was to demand that the Portuguese put the new peace treaty into effect or she would declare war. The Portuguese governor tried to throw Nzingha out of her country. The result was war.

Using her knowledge of the Europeans, their customs, and their religions, Nzingha was able to form powerful alliances, particularly with the Dutch who wanted to end Portuguese control over the slave trade in Africa. A shrewd leader, Nzingha was not only able to keep her country free from European control, she also tried to expand her kingdom as well. Queen Nzingha declared that all slaves who could reach Angola would be free.

After she died at the age of 81, her country finally fell into the hands of the Portuguese. Yet even today Queen Nzingha is an inspiring symbol of African resistance to white European domination.

Sojourner Truth

Freedom's Messenger
1797–1883
Birthplace: Hurley, New York

[T]he Lord gave me Truth, because I was to declare truth to the people.

Although Sojourner Truth was not allowed to learn to read or write, she was a wise woman and had an extraordinary gift of speech. Sojourner was born a slave named Isabella Baumfree. She was one of 12 children and was owned by several different slavemasters in New York State. Slavery was outlawed in New York in 1827, but her master would not free her, so Sojourner ran away with her youngest son.

Motivated by a religious vision, Sojourner, at the age of 46, left her home in New York City with 25 cents, a new dress, and a new name to start her own campaign against slavery. She chose the name Sojourner Truth because she planned to travel from place to place telling all who would listen the truth about slavery.

Sojourner, a powerful speaker, was often compared to another great African-American orator and abolitionist, Frederick Douglass. Feeling dejected about the condition of African Americans, Frederick once gave a gloomy speech that expressed little hope for the future. Sojourner rose and challenged him. "Frederick, is God dead?" she asked.

Some thought she had a mystical effect on her audience. But Sojourner maintained that she had strong beliefs in her causes and was determined to stand up for them. Even though she was often physically beaten for speaking out against slavery, this brave woman could not be stopped.

In 1863, Abraham Lincoln signed the Emancipation Proclamation, which outlawed slavery. But the Southern states did not recognize the law until they were defeated in the Civil War. During the war, Sojourner nursed wounded soldiers and the newly emancipated slaves. She asked President Lincoln to urge Northern free blacks to fight for the Union. She advised the freed slaves to get an education and to own land.

After the Civil War, Sojourner continued to fight for black equality and for women's rights. She dedicated her life to opening the doors of freedom to all people. Sojourner published her narrative in 1875 and died, at the age of 86, in Battle Creek, Michigan.

Harriet Tubman

Black Moses
c. 1820–1913
Birthplace: Dorchester County, Maryland

I never run my train off the track and I never lost a passenger.

T he small band of runaway slaves hid behind trees. They huddled together to hide from the cruel slave catchers. Would the runaways be caught and taken back to slavery? Or would they escape to freedom in the North?

"Not a sound from anyone!" a voice warned. It was Harriet Tubman. She knew well the risks and dangers they all faced. This trip to lead slaves from the South was not her first. As soon as the slave catchers were gone, the group of runaway slaves made their way through the dark woods and escaped to the North. "Black Moses" had struck again.

Harriet Tubman was born on a slave-breeding plantation in Maryland, one of 11 children. After the master of her plantation died, it was rumored that the slaves were to be sent to the Deep South. Fearing the consequences of such a move, Harriet and two of her brothers decided to escape. Afraid of what would happen if they were caught, her brothers turned back. But Harriet kept on walking to freedom.

Later, Harriet dared to return to the plantation to help three of her brothers and sisters escape. She returned again to free her mother and father. Using an established route called the "Underground Railroad," Harriet made 19 dangerous rescue trips to help other African Americans find the road to freedom. Along this route, friends and supporters provided safe hiding places, food, and clothing for the runaway slaves.

Angry slave masters offered a $40,000 reward for Harriet's capture, but she managed to fool them again and again. As a "conductor" on the "Underground Railroad," Harriet led more than 300 slaves to freedom and never lost a "passenger."

Harriet Tubman received many honors, including a medal from Queen Victoria of England. But this great fighter for freedom spent her last years in poverty. When she finally received a $20 monthly government pension for her nursing services during the Civil War, she used it to help establish a place for aged and needy freedmen.

Ellen Craft

Brave Runaway Slave
1826–1897
Birthplace: Clinton, Georgia

I had much rather starve in England, a free woman, than to be slave for the best man that ever breathed upon the American continent.

Ellen, the child of her mother's master, had such light skin that those who did not know she was a slave thought she was a member of the master's family. Ellen was not treated as badly as many of the other slaves, but the master's wife was so jealous that she took 11-year-old Ellen away from her mother and gave Ellen to her own daughter as a wedding present.

Being taken away from her mother changed Ellen. The ordeal made her realize that the life of a slave was bad no matter how well one was treated.

When Ellen got older, she married William Craft, another slave. He was a very talented carpenter and cabinetmaker. The couple spent many evenings discussing the problems of slavery. One night, William told Ellen of an idea he had: Since Ellen was often mistaken for a white person, she could disguise herself as his master, travel with William as her slave, and they could escape to the North together. Ellen agreed to try it.

Disguised as master and slave, Ellen and William traveled North by train from Georgia to Philadelphia. Ellen cut her hair short and dressed as a man. She wore green-tinted glasses to hide her eyes. She limped, wore her arm in a sling, covered her face with a bandage, and pretended to be hard of hearing and very ill. William explained to anyone who asked that his master was going to Philadelphia for better medical care.

The trip took four days, and at each stop along the way, the couple became more and more nervous. But they escaped successfully. When they arrived in Philadelphia, sympathetic abolitionists gave them shelter and protection from slave hunters until they could flee to England. There they started a family and learned to read and write. In 1860, William Craft wrote a very exciting book about their escape entitled *Running a Thousand Miles for Freedom.*

In 1868, after slavery was abolished, the Crafts and their five children returned to the United States, bought a plantation, and opened a trade school for African Americans.

Mary Church Terrell

Fighter for Women's Rights
1863–1954
Birthplace: Memphis, Tennessee

[K]eep on going—keep on insisting—keep on fighting injustice....

In a period of American history when most people felt that blacks and women were intellectually inferior to white men, Mary Eliza Church proved them wrong time and time again. The daughter of Robert Church, a former slave, Mary graduated from Oberlin College in Ohio in 1884. She majored in the classics, considered at that time a "gentlemen's" course of study. Four years later, she earned a master's degree in higher mathematics and went on to study abroad.

A strong women's rights advocate, Mary believed that women should work if they wanted to. Her father did not. He disinherited Mary because she went to Wilberforce, Ohio, to teach. When Mary married Robert Terrell, a judge, she moved with him to Washington. She was later appointed to the city's Board of Education. She was the first black woman in the United States to hold such a position.

In 1892, a lynch mob murdered one of Mary's friends. President Benjamin Harrison refused Mary's request to condemn lynching in his annual message to Congress. Thus began Mary's lifelong battle against racism and sexism.

Mary and white suffragette leaders Susan B. Anthony and Jane Addams campaigned tirelessly to win passage of the 19th Amendment to the Constitution, which gave women the right to vote. Then, during World War I, Mary helped organize the Women Wage-Earners Association to improve working conditions for black women. Later, she helped form the National Association of Colored Women (NACW) and the National Association for the Advancement of Colored People (NAACP).

Up until the day of her death, Mary battled racial injustice. In 1940, at age 77, she wrote her autobiography, *A Colored Woman in a White World*. Later, when the American Association of University Women refused to admit black women, Mary—at age 86—began a three-year fight to change that policy. At age 90, Mary Church Terrell could still be found leading picket lines to end segregation in restaurants in Washington, DC.

Ida B. Wells

A Warrior with Words
1869–1931
Birthplace: Holly Springs, Mississippi

Eternal vigilance is the price of liberty . . . .

I da B. Wells's parents were strong people who were born into slavery. By their example, they taught Ida courage and strength and an unwavering love of freedom. When Ida was 14, her parents and a brother died of yellow fever. After their deaths, Ida raised her five other brothers and sisters by herself and still managed to continue her education.

Even after slavery was outlawed, African Americans continued to suffer many injustices. Many families had their lands stolen. Many were murdered. Many African-American men were lynched—murdered by hanging—for crimes they did not commit. Ida was very angry about these cruelties and decided to do something about them. Using words as her weapons, Ida waged her own war.

After teaching school for six years and writing for a local black weekly newspaper, Ida decided to establish her own newspaper. As editor and co-owner of the weekly *Memphis Free Speech*, she attacked discrimination and prejudice on all fronts. She made people aware of how black people were suffering because of racial injustice.

Because her words told so much truth, some people wanted to silence Ida. She had to carry two pistols to protect herself, but soon that wasn't enough. In 1892, after revealing the truth about the lynching of three African-American businessmen by whites, Ida had to escape Memphis to save herself from a lynch mob. Ida went to New York where she wrote for the *New York Age*, a black weekly published by Thomas Fortune. Two years later, she published *A Red Record*, the first book to document the lynching of African Americans.

Ida was one of the most militant journalists of her era. She wrote for publications such as the *Indianapolis World*, *Little Rock Sun*, and *Detroit Plain Dealer* and her demands for justice mobilized many women to actively organize themselves.

Ida's antilynching campaign took her on lecture tours all over the country and to England. She became secretary of the National Afro-American Council and later founded the Negro Fellowship League. Like Mary Church Terrell, Ida was also a founding member of the National Association for the Advancement of Colored People.

Amy-Jacques Garvey

Black Nationalist
1896–1973
Birthplace: Jamaica, West Indies

*Stand on your own two black feet and fight
like hell for your place in the world....*

Amy-Jacques came from a family of proud, educated business people. The biggest influence in her early life was her dad, a stern but kind man who taught her to be independent. He wanted Amy to have a good education too, so as soon as she could read, her father would sit her down every Sunday with a dictionary and make her read newspapers in foreign languages!

By 1919, Amy was living in New York City, but she had no job and had just been evicted from her apartment. By coincidence, she met another Amy—Amy Ashwood, who was engaged to be married to Marcus Garvey and was his secretary. Out of sympathy, Amy Ashwood invited Amy-Jacques to live with her.

Marcus Garvey was a famous Jamaican who had started the Universal Negro Improvement Association (UNIA). This organization tried to bring together the world's African peoples through racial pride and economic power. Garvey had millions of black followers all over the world. Many members of UNIA built their own factories and businesses, including a steamship company.

At first, Amy-Jacques had no real interest in UNIA, but she became Garvey's secretary after his marriage to Amy Ashwood. She soon became indispensable to Garvey. It wasn't long before Garvey fell in love with Amy-Jacques. He divorced Amy Ashwood and married Amy-Jacques in 1922.

That same year Marcus Garvey was arrested and convicted on charges of mail fraud. Eventually, he was convicted of treason and even though he was later pardoned, he served two years of a five-year sentence. During those years Amy worked to keep her husband's message alive. Not only did she raise money for his defense, she also wrote for UNIA's publications, and edited and published a book about Marcus Garvey's philosophy.

Although Marcus Garvey struggled to rebuild UNIA in Jamaica, he was considered a political threat. The pressures caused him to move to London, where he died in 1940. After his death, Amy-Jacques remained active in black nationalist work and continued to write on the subject until she died in Jamaica in 1973.

Queen Mother Moore

Revolutionary and Organizer
1898–
Birthplace: New Iberia, Louisiana

My bones are tired. Not tired of struggling, but tired of oppression.

As a child, Audley Moore learned about the oppression of African Americans from the tragic things that happened to her own family. Her great-grandmother, an African woman who was enslaved, had been raped by her master. Audley's grandfather was lynched right in front of her grandmother, leaving her with five children. These events motivated Audley to devote her life to fighting racism.

Although Audley was only able to complete the third grade, she was very interested in any activity that promoted unity among black people. In the early 1920s, she became a member of Marcus Garvey's Universal Negro Improvement Association and supported his "Back to Africa" movement. When Garvey himself came to New Orleans, but was not permitted to speak in public, Audley and 3,500 armed blacks marched to City Hall and demanded that he be allowed to speak.

But Audley didn't just join groups, she formed groups. She became well known in Louisiana as a community leader and organizer. Among the many organizations she founded was the Universal Association of Ethiopian Women, Inc. The activities of this group restored 23,000 families to the welfare rolls, and saved several African-American men from execution in Louisiana.

Audley always hated the term "Negro" to label people of African descent. She felt that the word "African" should be used to describe her people. So she founded the African American Cultural Foundation, Inc., which led the fight against the word "Negro." She also organized groups to assist in the defense of the Scottsboro Boys. These nine black youths had been wrongly accused of raping two white girls in the 1930s.

Even when Audley later moved to Harlem, she stayed involved in civil rights causes. In 1930, she organized the first rent strikes there.

For over 80 years Audley has fought for the rights of all African peoples. She has won many awards for her work. In the 1950s, a group of admiring African students gave her the appropriate title of "Queen Mother."

Ella Baker

Lifelong Civil Rights Activist
1903–1986
Birthplace: Norfolk, Virginia

People have to be made to understand that they cannot look for salvation anywhere but to themselves.

T o document Ella Baker's life is to recount the history of the civil rights movement. Whenever there was a cause to fight for or a group to organize, this dedicated woman was there.

Ella grew up and received her education in North Carolina. Upon graduating from Shaw University, she moved to New York City just before the Depression of 1929. There she became active in various causes. She worked briefly with the Work Projects Administration (WPA) and then worked to end discrimination in organized labor through the NAACP. Ella was very involved with the NAACP as an organizer, an education director, and, at one time, president of the New York branch.

Ella went South in the 1950s to help the civil rights movement as it was developing in Alabama. With 30 years of organizing experience under her belt, Ella's advice to Martin Luther King, Jr. and the other leaders of the Montgomery bus boycott in 1955 was invaluable. She stayed South and helped Dr. King set up the headquarters of the Southern Christian Leadership Conference (SCLC). A few years later she played an important part in helping to organize the student sit-in demonstrations that were occurring all over the South. This activity led to the formation of the Student Nonviolent Coordinating Committee (SNCC), one of the most powerful student-activist movements formed in U.S. history. She also helped to found the Mississippi Freedom Democratic Party in 1964, which helped to give African Americans in Mississippi more political power.

Ella continued to serve as the "godmother" and mentor of SNCC as it moved into other human rights issues. Her greatest asset was her ability to organize and mobilize people of all generations. Although her name was not publicized as much as other male leaders, the civil rights movement would not have been the same without her.

Shortly before her death in 1986, a documentary titled "*Fundi*: The Story of Ella Baker" was aired on public television. *Fundi* is the Swahili word for a person who passes on skills to a younger generation. It is a fitting description of Ella Baker's legacy.

Clara McBride Hale

"Mother Hale"
1905–1992
Birthplace: Philadelphia, Pennsylvania

Until I die, I'm going to keep doing. My people need me. . . . I'm not an American hero. I'm a person who loves children.

Clara McBride grew up in a house full of children. Her mother not only watched out for her own four children, but the neighbor's children as well. She taught them all to be strong, proud, and self-confident.

So it's no wonder that Clara loved children. When Clara's husband died, leaving her with a son and daughter to care for, she started making her living watching other people's children. Some of the children didn't want to leave Clara's home to go back to their own parents, so Clara kept them and raised them as her own. Over the years Clara has raised 40 children and sent them all to college. Many are now doctors, lawyers, ministers, and teachers, and Clara is proud of all of them.

In 1969, "Mother Hale" decided to stop taking in babies. But then she began to care for a young mother with an addicted baby. Because some expectant mothers are drug addicts or infected with the deadly disease called AIDS, their babies are born with an addiction or with the disease. It wasn't long before Clara had 22 addicted babies living in her five-room apartment. The number didn't stop at 22, however. In 1973, Mother Hale founded Hale House in Harlem to help more babies born to drug addicts. Soon she also started nursing babies with AIDS.

Over 600 addicted babies have been cared for at Hale House. From the loving care they received there, these children have returned to good health. Clara's children with AIDS were less fortunate. Because there is no cure for the disease, most babies with AIDS will die young. But Mother Hale was commited to caring for these children. "I want them to live a good life while they can and know someone loves them," she said.

For her dedication to helping others, Mother Hale received the 16th Annual Truman Award. In 1985, President Reagan cited her as an "American hero."

Dorothy Irene Height

Champion of Youth Activism
1912–
Birthplace: Richmond, Virginia

We are geared toward helping young people to understand. . .that they are bound to grow as they try to tackle real problems.

 o one is too young to fight for civil rights, and events in Dorothy Height's life underscore that fact. While she was a high school student, she was a finalist in a speech-making contest. Her speech was about peace. Just before she made that speech in the final contest, she was denied entry into a hotel because of her race. She quickly rewrote her speech and compared her experience with that of Mary and Joseph when they were denied entry into the inn on the night of Jesus' birth. The point was well taken; Dorothy won the contest.

Trained as a social worker, Dorothy worked as a caseworker in the New York City Department of Welfare before becoming involved in the National Council of Negro Women (NCNW), an organization founded by Mary McLeod Bethune in 1935. In addition to fighting for equality for black women, the NCNW focused on issues that included child labor, minimum wage, and people's working conditions. After Mary McLeod Bethune recruited her to help set up her organization, Dorothy quickly became deeply involved. She was made its president in 1957, a position she holds to this day.

Under Dorothy's guidance, the NCNW has not only sponsored special training sessions, conferences, and career meetings for young people, it has also worked on such problems as inadequate education and teen pregnancy. In addition, it has achieved many of its other goals, including the erection of the Bethune Memorial statue, the first monument to an African American ever erected in a public park in Washington, D.C.

Dorothy has fulfilled Mary McLeod Bethune's dream of a national organization. Now the NCNW is trying to strengthen the black community by recognizing its historical, traditional, and cultural values. In 1986, Dorothy Height founded the "Black Family Reunion Celebration" designed to counter the negative images of black life that were depicted by a national television special. Supported by the NCNW, the Reunion has become a successful annual event.

Rosa Parks

Mother of the Movement
1913–
Birthplace: Tuskegee, Alabama

*When people made up their minds that they
wanted to be free and took action, then there
was a change. But they couldn't rest on just
that change. It has to continue.*

I t was just weeks before Christmas in 1955 in Montgomery, Alabama. People were rushing home after a hard day at work. Forty-two-year-old Rosa Parks was one of them. She had had a busy day at her tailoring job.

When the bus arrived, all the seats were quickly taken. Since black people were only allowed to sit in the back of the bus (the front section was reserved for whites), Rosa sat in the "colored" section, as usual. But on this day, the bus was crowded and a white man had to stand. So the bus driver ordered Rosa and several other African Americans to give up their seats to the whites. Rosa refused. The police were called and she was arrested.

Rosa Parks's refusal to give up her seat sparked a movement against segregation in Montgomery that started with a 381-day bus boycott by African Americans. The leader of that movement was a young minister named Dr. Martin Luther King, Jr., in whose church the boycott was organized. Dr. King called Rosa "the great fuse that led to the modern stride toward freedom." Her actions on the bus that day guaranteed her place in history.

Some people think Rosa's stand in 1955 was her first effort to face up to discrimination and segregation. It was not. Rosa was a member of the Montgomery branch of the NAACP and served as its secretary. Twelve years earlier, she had also refused to go to the back of the bus and had been forced to get off.

After she was arrested in 1955, however, Rosa and her family paid a big price for her courage. As a result of the successful boycott, she and her husband lost their jobs. They subsequently moved to Detroit, Michigan, because they no longer felt safe in Montgomery.

Rosa still lives in Detroit. For 25 years she served as administrative assistant to Representative John Conyers of Michigan. Her first book, *Rosa Parks*, written with James Haskins, will be published in 1992. Through her speaking engagements, Rosa Parks continues to inspire the people of America.

Fannie Lou Hamer

Sharecropper/Civil Rights Activist
1917–1977
Birthplace: Montgomery County,
Mississippi

The special plight and the role of black women is not something that just happened three years ago. We've had a special plight for 350 years.

F annie Lou Hamer had been a cotton sharecropper all of her life. She began to pick cotton at the age of six, so tending the cotton fields was all she was trained to do. Day after day, with her husband and her two children, she worked the very same plantation on which she was raised—until August 31, 1962.

On that day Fannie Lou Hamer walked into the registrar's office in Indianola, Mississippi, and demanded that she be allowed to register to vote. On that day, Fannie Lou Hamer was no longer a humble sharecropper. Fannie Lou Hamer had become a civil rights activist.

Because she had tried to register, she and her family were forced to leave their home on the plantation that very evening. They went to a friend's house. Ten days later, 16 bullets were fired into that house.

Despite the violence that was a reaction to her courageous act, once Fannie had decided to take control of her own life, nothing would stop her. She was "sick and tired of being sick and tired," and she was going to change things. She joined groups of civil rights activists and quickly became a leader who organized an aggressive strategy to change Mississippi's racist political system.

In 1964, Fannie cofounded the Council of Federated Organizations, which recruited Northern white students to protest the treatment of African Americans in the South. She helped set up the Mississippi Freedom Democratic Party to challenge the white-ruled regular Democratic party and secure more equal representation of blacks in Mississippi politics.

Fannie Lou Hamer was one of the 20 children born to her sharecropping parents. She was also partially disabled by polio and had very little formal education. But her spirit gave her something no college degree could provide: the determination to face centuries of Southern white oppression and demand that it end.

Coretta Scott King

Keeper of the Flame
1927–
Birthplace: Marion, Alabama

I was, and still am, convinced that the women of the world, united without any regard for national or racial dimensions, can become a most powerful force for international peace and brotherhood.

C oretta Scott grew up, the second of three children, in a fairly well-to-do family in Perry County, Alabama. Because her father was a successful landowner, he often had a lot of trouble with the local whites, so Coretta knew well what white resentment and bigotry were like.

An excellent student, Coretta was also very interested in music, so with the help of a "race relations" scholarship, she went to Antioch College in Ohio. Intending to pursue a singing career, Coretta then won a fellowship at Boston's New England Conservatory of Music. She worked at a variety of menial jobs while she studied for her music degree. It was in Boston where she met a young minister from Atlanta who was studying for his doctorate in philosophy and theology—Martin Luther King, Jr. They were married in 1953. Little did Coretta know then that her life would never be the same.

It was two years after their marriage that Dr. King became involved in the Montgomery bus boycott. His actions at that time turned him into a prominent civil rights leader. He became the voice of the nonviolent civil rights movement and was hailed by 18 million African Americans as their key spokesperson. Throughout all of Martin's struggles as a civil rights leader, Coretta stood by his side, supporting him. Even when their home was bombed, Coretta was strong.

But never was she stronger than when Martin was assassinated on April 4, 1968. The entire world mourned his death, and it was up to Coretta to provide comfort. She continued to preach Martin's message for nonviolent social change, even while she held in her own grief and consoled their four children.

Since 1968, Coretta has continued to be active as a human rights leader. She is president of the Martin Luther King, Jr. Center for Nonviolent Social Change in Atlanta, Georgia. In 1984, she became chairperson of the Martin Luther King, Jr. Federal Holiday Commission.

Winnie Mandela

**The Incarnation of the African Spirit
1936–
Birthplace: Pondoland, Transkei,
      South Africa**

*There is only one person who is oppressed in
this country. He is black . . . . [U]prisings are
bound to be the order of the day, because our
struggle here has been reduced by the white
man, by his choice, to black versus white.*

Winnie Mandela is one of nine children. Her Xhosa name is Nkosikazi Nobandle
Nomzamo Madikizela, but her father added "Winifred" to her name. Even though both
of her parents were teachers, her family was very poor and was forced to live under the
inhumane conditions of apartheid (the racial segregation policy of South Africa).

Winnie, like all black people of South Africa, knew that whites believed they were superior
to blacks. She wanted to help change things so that her people would be recognized and treated
as equals. Receiving top grades in her studies, Winnie became South Africa's first black
medical social worker. In the course of her work she would hear about black resistance
campaigns being led by the African National Congress (ANC) and a lawyer named Nelson
Mandela. It was when Nelson was on trial for treason in 1956 that Winnie met him through
friends. She fell in love with him immediately and they were married. But life with an activist
was hard. "Life with him was life without him," Winnie has said. Nelson was constantly
harassed and arrested by the security police. When he was finally convicted of treason, he was
sentenced to life in prison.

During the 27 years that Nelson was imprisoned, Winnie became a hero of the anti-
apartheid movement. She became determined to fight back, and her tactics were often
criticized for their militancy.

When Nelson was released in 1990, the world watched in expectation Winnie's reunion with
him. The marriage was not to last. Winnie's involvement with a group of militant youths and
her subsequent conviction on charges of kidnapping and assault strained relations with both
her husband and the ANC. The Mandelas divorced in 1991, and Winnie was discredited.

Some say Winnie became a victim of the struggle, but there is no doubt that black South
Africans would not have achieved their independence without her strength and leadership.

Marian Wright Edelman

Fighter for Children's Rights
1939–
Birthplace: Bennettsville, South Carolina

The outside world told black kids when I was growing up that we weren't worth anything . . . . But our parents said it wasn't so and our churches and our school teachers said it wasn't so. They believed in us and we, therefore, believed in ourselves.

As a child of a minister father who started the first black home for senior citizens in South Carolina, Marian learned that no one was too young to help others. Service was of the highest value, she was taught. That belief has characterized her life and has motivated Marian to aid those less fortunate people of the world, particularly children and the poor.

After she attended Spelman College in Atlanta, the University of Paris, France, and the University of Geneva, Switzerland, Marian received her law degree from Yale Law School. She became the first black woman admitted to the bar in Mississippi. Marian then did civil rights work with the NAACP, directing that organization's Legal Defense and Education Fund in Mississippi and New York.

In 1968, she left her law practice to work toward a better future for American children. She became so concerned about the welfare of children that she organized the Children's Defense Fund in 1973. As president of the group, Marian speaks on behalf of children and their families about health, welfare, youth employment, and legal rights issues.

In her book, *Families in Peril: An Agenda for Social Change*, Marian makes powerful statements about the appalling situation of America's children, black and white. She urges support for poor mothers and children of all races. Her ultimate goal is to establish a quality child-care system that will give children the sense of security and belonging they need to become loving, productive adults.

Among the many awards Marian has received for her work are the Outstanding Leadership Award from the National Women's Political Caucus and Black Caucus, 1980; the Roy Wilkins Civil Rights Award from the NAACP, 1984; and the prestigious MacArthur Fellowship in 1985. These awards—and all the others she has received—testify to the high regard and respect Marian Edelman has earned in her commitment to our country's future citizens.

Angela Yvonne Davis

Political Activist and Academician
1944–
Birthplace: Birmingham, Alabama

To recognize ourselves as being especially oppressed because we are African Americans does not mean that we cannot also join hands with those from other racial communities, national communities. . . .

Angela Davis grew up in segregated Birmingham, Alabama. Her neighborhood was called "Dynamite Hill" because of all the bombings against black people that took place there. Her parents were active in civil rights and in politics, so Angela's activism grew naturally out of her childhood experiences.

An exceptional student, Angela received her undergraduate degree from Brandeis University in Massachusetts. She studied further in Europe, and then received her master's degree from the University of California at San Diego.

Angela was always concerned about the plight of her people. She worked with SNCC, the Black Panthers, and eventually joined a Communist party because she felt a need to "relate the struggle for the liberation of black people to the working-class struggles of people of all racial backgrounds."

As a result of her activism on the part of African-American prisoners, Angela was implicated in what was called the Soledad Brothers' shootout in 1970. She was charged with conspiracy, murder, and kidnapping. The Federal Bureau of Investigation put her on its most-wanted list. When she was captured, Angela was put in jail without bail.

Many Americans all across the country were outraged by the government's actions. A "Free Angela" movement quickly grew to help her win her release. In 1972, after 16 months in prison, Angela was acquitted and set free.

Because of her activism and her outspoken beliefs about civil, human, and women's rights, Angela Davis has become a powerful symbol for many Americans. Now she teaches women's studies and ethnic studies at San Francisco State University. She is co-chairperson of the National Alliance Against Racist and Political Repression and works with the Black Women's Health Project. She has written important articles on racism and feminism, including her autobiography and *Women, Race and Class*, and she continues to speak out against oppression in whatever form it takes.

Educators

BUILDING STRONG FOUNDATIONS

Marva Collins teaches young students at Chicago's Westside Preparatory School.

Thousands will tell you
that it cannot be done,
thousands will tell you
that you will fail.
But only you child
will know how far you can sail,
So say to yourself,
"I shall not fail."

—Marva N. Collins

Fannie Jackson Coppin

Trailblazer for Black Education
1836–1913
Birthplace: Washington, D.C.

[I]n my classes. . . I felt that I had the honor of the whole African race upon my shoulders. I felt that, should I fail, it would be ascribed to the fact that I was colored. . . .

Fannie's grandfather purchased freedom for himself and four of his six children, but he could not save enough money to buy the freedom of Fannie's mother, Lucy. So Fannie Jackson was born a slave. However, Fannie's aunt, Sarah Clark, was so impressed with her smart young niece that she became determined to free the little girl. Sarah worked for six dollars a month for almost two years to save the $125 she needed to buy Fannie's freedom.

Once Fannie was free, she was sent to live with another aunt in Massachusetts. Later she went to work for the Calvert family in Rhode Island, where she also attended school. Her drive to get an education was so strong that Fannie left the Calvert family, with whom she was very happy, to attend Rhode Island State Normal School and then Oberlin College in Ohio.

All during this time, Fannie's aunt Sarah continued to support her, and Fannie did not disappoint her loving guardian. At Oberlin, she organized classes for newly freed slaves, gave private music lessons, and became the college's first black student-teacher. When she graduated, she became one of the first African-American women in the United States to receive a college degree.

After graduating, Fannie was immediately hired by the Institute for Colored Youth in Philadelphia (now called Cheyney University) in 1865. Four years later she became its principal and established a successful teaching program to help young African Americans prepare for different trades. Later in her life, Fannie married Reverend Levi J. Coppin, who asked his new wife to give up teaching. Fannie refused. She did, however, get involved with missionary work, and often traveled with her husband.

Just before her death in 1913, Fannie wrote her autobiography, *Reminiscences of School Life*, and *Hints on Teaching*. Coppin State College, which is located in Baltimore, Maryland, was named in honor of Fannie, the former slave who became a dedicated teacher.

Charlotte Forten Grimké

Quiet but Courageous
1837–1914
Birthplace: Philadelphia, Pennsylvania

I wish some of those persons at the North who say the race is hopelessly and naturally inferior could see the readiness with which these children, so long oppressed and deprived of every privilege, learn and understand.

U nlike most blacks living in the 1800s, Charlotte Forten was born free and wealthy. But even wealth could not buy her equality. Because she was black, the schools in Philadelphia refused to admit her, so she was tutored at home until she was 16. Then she went to Salem, Massachusetts to attend the integrated schools there. She lived with Charles Remond, an abolitionist, and his family.

Charlotte was an outstanding student who taught herself French, German, and Latin. Her diary shows that she read over 100 books, ranging from the classics to poetry, in one year. In 1856, at age 19, Charlotte graduated with honors from Salem Normal School and began teaching at Epes Grammar School, also in Salem. There she became the first African American to teach white people in Massachusetts. When she was not teaching, Charlotte spent much of her time working for antislavery causes. She also enjoyed writing.

With the outbreak of the Civil War, some slaves in the South fled for safety to the Sea Islands off the coast of South Carolina. When the government began recruiting young people to teach the former slaves living there, Charlotte volunteered her services. She was one of the first black teachers to be a part of the movement to teach ex-slaves.

Life was not easy on the Sea Islands, but Charlotte didn't give up. She knew that education was the best weapon for fighting prejudice and oppression. When she left the Sea Islands in 1864, thousands of children were enrolled in the schools and just as many adults were learning to read. Charlotte recorded her experiences in her personal journal, which was not published until 1953.

Charlotte continued to teach until 1873, when she became a clerk in the U.S. Treasury Department. She married Reverend Francis J. Grimké in 1878.

Although physically frail and sensitive, Charlotte had great courage. She gave up a comfortable life in the North to help the destitute people of the Sea Islands, thus showing a deep concern for the welfare of her people.

Lucy Craft Laney

A Loving Educator
1854–1933
Birthplace: Macon, Georgia

Black women are the regenerative force to uplift the black race.

Lucy Laney was born a slave, the seventh of ten children. It was against the law to educate slaves, but a very unusual thing happened to Lucy: her master's sister taught her to read and write. Lucy not only attended high school, but she was able to enter Atlanta University with the help of that kind woman.

After graduating from college at the age of 19, Lucy spent ten years teaching public school in Savannah and Augusta, Georgia. During those years, she found that she was particularly good at motivating the difficult students.

Although she loved teaching, public school was too limiting for Lucy, so she was pleased when she heard that the Presbyterian Church was about to open a private school. She accepted their invitation to be the teacher there. The problem was that there was no money, only a room in which to hold the classes. Lucy was excited about the opportunity, but she knew she would have to work hard to keep the school going.

Knowing how difficult it was for black students to get into college, Lucy decided that her students would be well prepared. Her school soon became very popular, but there was always a struggle for enough money to run it. Lucy traveled all over the country giving lectures to help raise money. She sacrificed her own personal comforts for those of her students. Many people were impressed by Lucy's efforts and helped her. Francina E. H. Haines, in particular, helped raise much of the money for the school. The school was named Haines Normal and Industrial Institute in her honor.

Because of Lucy's dedication, many of her students went on to good colleges and became teachers and other civic leaders. By 1931, the school had trained or prepared over 700 students and 27 teachers—including Mary McLeod Bethune, who began her teaching career at Haines in the early 1900s.

Lucy Laney died on October 23, 1933. Sixteen years later, Haines Institute was forced to close. But Lucy Laney is not forgotten: her portrait still hangs in the Georgia State House in Atlanta. One of Lucy's obituaries stated: "Lucy Laney was great because she loved people. She believed all God's children had wings. . ."

Mary McLeod Bethune

The Great Educator
1875–1955
Birthplace: Maysville, South Carolina

I am my mother's daughter, and the drums of Africa still beat in my heart. They will not let me rest while there is a single Negro boy or girl without a chance to prove his worth.

When Mary was a child growing up in the cotton fields of South Carolina, many people thought education was a waste of time for African-American children. But Mary was eager to go to school, and even though it was difficult, her parents supported her.

Mary proved to be a hard-working pupil. In 1895, she graduated from Moody Bible Institute, where she was the only black student. She then began teaching school at Haines Institute in Georgia. But then Mary heard about a city in Florida where there was no school, and in 1904 she headed to Daytona Beach to establish a school for young black women.

When Mary arrived in Daytona, she had only $1.50 in her pocket. But the lack of money didn't stop her. She taught her first five students out of a rented cottage. She sold sweet potato pies and asked for donations from churches and clubs to finance her struggle. People responded to this determined woman. With their help and a lot of hard work, Mary was able to build the Daytona Normal and Industrial Institute for Negro Girls. In 1923, she merged her school with another black Florida school, the Cookman Institute. The result was Bethune-Cookman College, now a highly regarded accredited academic institution.

Mary McLeod Bethune used her stubborn determination to help make education available to thousands of African Americans. She called on that same quality to fight for other causes as well. She founded the National Council of Negro Women (NCNW) in 1935 and was the director of the National Business League and the National Urban League. She was also an advisor to four presidents.

In 1935, President Franklin D. Roosevelt established the Office of Minority Affairs and appointed Mary as administrator. It was the first post of its kind to be assigned to an African-American woman. Later, her title was changed to director of the Division of Negro Affairs.

Mary McLeod Bethune lived for 80 years. During most of that time she worked tirelessly to help her people, and her legacy lives on.

Septima Poinsette Clark

Founder of Freedom Schools
1898–1987
Birthplace: Charleston, South Carolina

I have great belief in the fact that whenever there is chaos, it creates wonderful thinking. I consider chaos a gift.

Septima's mother was raised in Haiti, where she was taught to read and write. Her mother was extremely proud of these skills, so she planted in Septima the belief that literacy was the key to power.

After graduating from high school at 18, Septima was made the principal of a school for black children. The school had only two teachers to instruct 132 students from kindergarten through eighth grade. Septima had no teaching experience, but she became committed to her students and to her profession.

While she taught, Septima continued her own education, and received her master's degree. At the same time, she tried to help black teachers get better jobs and better pay. Because of this work, and because she refused to withdraw her membership in the NAACP, the Charleston Board of Education fired her in 1956 and denied her 30 years worth of retirement pay.

This did not stop Septima. She went on to become the director of education at the Highlander Folk School in Tennessee and also helped organize schools to teach poor Southern blacks how to read and write. These soon became known as citizenship schools.

At the citizenship schools, black people also learned about the United States Constitution. They learned that democracy meant equal treatment for all people. They learned that one of the ways to make their voices heard was to vote. At that time, most Southern blacks were not able to vote because they had to pass a literacy test before they could register. Septima taught them how to pass this test at her citizenship schools.

Septima traveled all over the South recruiting hundreds of teachers for these schools. She always traveled by bus and refused to sit in the "colored" sections in the back. Eventually she became actively involved with Martin Luther King's Southern Christian Leadership Conference. Her citizenship schools became known as Freedom Schools during the civil rights movement of the 1960s.

Because of Septima Clark's tireless commitment to her people, thousands of African Americans learned how to read, to write, and to stand up for their rights.

Daisy Bates

Fighter for Desegregation
1914–
Birthplace: Huttig, Arkansas

*I don't think I was courageous. I think I was
determined.*

One night, when Daisy was a baby, her mother was killed by three white men. When her father went to look for her mother, he left Daisy with his best friend. "Keep her until I come back," he said. But he never came back, so her father's friend adopted the baby girl.

This was Daisy's first experience with the brutalities of racism, but it was not her last. During her childhood Daisy had to face many instances of racial injustice, which made her very angry. Her anger was so great that her adopted father's dying words to her were, "If you're going to hate, make it count for something. Hate segregation in the South."

So Daisy turned her anger into action. With her husband, L.C. Bates, she established the *Arkansas State Press*, a weekly newspaper, in the early 1940s. Then Daisy was elected president of the Arkansas NAACP. This was when she took her father's words to heart and actively fought for the desegregation of public schools.

In 1957, African-American children were not allowed to attend the same schools as white children in Little Rock, Arkansas. But despite threats to their lives, Daisy and nine brave black students set out to integrate the town's Central High School.

This upset many white people, including the governor of Arkansas, who used state guardsmen to try to stop the children. When one of the students, Elizabeth Eckford, tried to enter the high school alone, she faced the bayonets of the guardsmen and a hate-filled white mob that screamed, "Get her! Drag her over to this tree! Lynch her!"

Elizabeth escaped with the help of two white friends, but the rest of the country was deeply shocked when that scene was shown on television. As a result, President Eisenhower sent in federal troops who protected Daisy and the children as they marched past the angry mobs and successfully integrated Central High. For their courage and perseverance, Daisy and the Little Rock Nine were awarded the NAACP Spingarn Medal.

In 1990, Daisy was awarded the Arkansas Citizen of the Year Award for her achievements.

Jean Blackwell Hutson

**Curator of the Schomburg Center for
Research in Black Culture
1914–
Birthplace: Summerfield, Florida**

Books are tools of self-education.

When Jean Blackwell was 22, she applied for a job at a public library in Baltimore, but was told that there were no more positions open for black people. So she went to New York City. There she found a job in Harlem at an exciting place: the Division of Negro Literature, History and Prints at the 135th Street Branch of the New York Public Library. This library was run by an African-American scholar named Arthur Schomburg. Told all of his life that black people had no history, Arthur Schomburg began collecting proof that they did, and he donated his collection to the library so that everyone could see it.

Working late one night, Jean decided to rearrange a section of the library's books according to the standard Dewey decimal system. Discovering what she had done the next day, Mr. Schomburg became furious. He had arranged the books by his own personal system of size and color! He was so angry at Jean that he fired her. Even after his death two years later she didn't go back to the library.

Ten years later, however, Jean accepted a temporary position as a librarian at the library, which was now named the Schomburg Center for Research in Black Culture. This "temporary" position lasted for 36 years. During this time, Jean helped build the Schomburg into a strong collection and became the center's acting director and then its curator.

Many social changes affected the African-American community during Jean's years at the Schomburg: school integration, the bus boycotts, the civil rights and black power movements of the 1960s. Jean was instrumental in acquiring many of the important books and papers that came out of those times. As a resident of Harlem, she also urged her community to help preserve their own history by sending their materials to the library. The Schomburg is now considered to be the most complete collection of materials that document the history and culture of peoples of African descent. And its doors are open—for free—to all who seek such knowledge.

Marva Nettles Collins

A Devoted Teacher
1936–
Birthplace: Monroeville, Alabama

*I don't want to be wealthy. I don't need that
kind of power. Power is when I walk into this
school and these little kids' eyes hold wonder
like a cup.*

Marva's childhood in Alabama was full of love and security. She had a close friendship with her father, and her family environment was strong and nurturing. It is this kind of love and security that Marva wants to pass on to the students at her Westside Preparatory School in Chicago.

Frustrated with the educational system that she worked in as a public school teacher for 14 years, Marva decided to take matters into her own hands and do things her own way. So in 1975, she took her retirement money and opened Westside Preparatory right in her home. At that time she had 18 students, including her own children. But her class grew quickly when Marva became known for her ability to help children who were labeled "learning disabled," "unteachable," or "retarded" by the public school system. Today Westside Preparatory occupies two buildings and has an enrollment of 250 students.

"Entrance to learn, exit to serve" is the school's motto, and each student is encouraged to follow it. Each student, for example, has to tutor five other children in their neighborhood. With such guidance, love, and firm discipline, Marva has successfully taught many children who could not be reached by other teachers. Those "unteachable" children were soon reciting Plato and Shakespeare, and scoring higher on their standardized tests than most public school students.

Marva's achievements were the subject of a 1981 television movie called "The Marva Collins Story," starring Cicely Tyson. All of the proceeds from that movie have gone into supporting Marva's school. Today teachers from all over the world visit Westside Preparatory to learn Marva's successful teaching methods.

Marva had a vision of educating children from the tough neighborhoods of Chicago. She has realized that dream and the students at her school are receiving the love, security, and the quality education that are theirs by right.

Mary Hatwood Futrell

Fighter for Quality Education
1940–
Birthplace: Alta Vista, Virginia

*Don't allow circumstances to hold you back —
even negative ones. You don't have to let your
circumstances define you. You can define
yourself, and the best way to find yourself is
through education.*

Mary was raised in Lynchburg, Virginia, the second child in a single-parent home. Even though she grew up in poverty, education was a high priority in her family and in her community. Mary's favorite hobby was reading. She would often sneak off into a hiding place and spend hours reading mystery novels, while her mother looked for her.

Mary's mother did not graduate from high school, but she did instill in her children a love of learning that would never die. The teachers at Mary's all-black high school also believed deeply in their students and insisted on high standards for Mary.

Although she was an excellent student and was active in many school activities, Mary never thought about college because her family had no money to send her. But when her teachers saw that she was scoring very high on her tests, they went out into the community and asked for donations for Mary. Then, on the night of her high school graduation, they presented Mary with the money. She was so surprised and grateful that she vowed then and there that she would somehow pay her people back.

Not only did Mary go on to get a bachelor's degree and a master's degree in education, she more than fulfilled the promise she made that night. She worked as a secondary school teacher for 20 years, and has held a number of important positions in educational organizations. She was president of the Education Association of Alexandria, Virginia, president of the Virginia Education Association, and served on the National Education Association (NEA) board of directors. She became the NEA's president in 1983. Mary has received numerous honorary doctorates and many awards and honors for her distinguished service as an educator.

Mary is presently the president of the World Confederation of Organizations of the Teaching Profession and a consultant for the Quality Education for Minorities Network. She takes care of her family, continues to teach, and is also a full-time student herself. She is studying for her doctorate in educational policy. But in the midst of all of her activities and accomplishments, Mary Futrell's most favorite hobby is still reading mystery novels!

Writers & Fine Artists

THE POWER OF CREATIVITY

Lift Every Voice and Sing, sculpture by Augusta Savage, 1939.

You may write me down in history
With your bitter, twisted lies,
You may trod me in the very dirt
But still, like dust, I'll rise.

—Maya Angelou

Phillis Wheatley

A Poet for Her Times
1753–1784
Birthplace: Senegal, West Africa

. . . I young in life, by seeming cruel fate
Was snatch'd from Afri's fancy'd happy feet:
What pangs excruciating must molest,
What sorrows labour in my parent's breast?...

P hillis was only eight years old when she was stolen from her parents in Africa and brought to America. She would never forget her family, her homeland, or her trip on the horrible slave ship. But Phillis was more fortunate than many other slaves. She was bought by John Wheatley, a Northern white merchant, and even though she had to do whatever the Wheatleys asked, they treated Phillis well.

The Wheatleys soon realized that Phillis was a very special child. Unlike most slavemasters, who wanted to keep their slaves illiterate, the Wheatleys taught Phillis to read and write. After only 16 months in America, Phillis was able to read even the most difficult parts of the Bible. By the time she was 14, she had written her first poem.

Soon, many people began to read her poetry. One of her poems, which was dedicated to George Washington, brought her much attention. Then, when Phillis was 20, she took ill, so the Wheatleys freed her from slavery and sent her to England to get better. While she was there, a London publishing company printed her first volume of verse, *Poems on Various Subjects, Religious and Moral.*

Phillis returned to America to nurse John Wheatley's wife and then the rest of the Wheatley family, who quickly fell ill and died within a few years. Phillis later married John Peters, a freed slave. He wound up in debtor's prison, but not before he had stolen the manuscript of her second book, which was never published. Phillis, forced to do hard work in a cheap boarding house, took ill and died at the young age of 31.

Although her life was short, Phillis Wheatley will always be remembered as one of America's first black poets.

Frances Ellen Watkins Harper

Black Woman Intellectual
1825–1911
Birthplace: Baltimore, Maryland

Through weary, wasting years men have destroyed, dashed in pieces, and overthrown, but today we stand on the threshold of woman's era, and woman's work is grandly constructive.

F rances Ellen Watkins was born of free parents in the North and was educated in a school run by her uncle. As a young girl, she started her literary career writing poetry. Her first collection of poems, *Forest Leaves*, was published when she was 20 years old. Her volume of verse entitled *Poems on Miscellaneous Subjects* (1854) sold 10,000 copies in the first five years of publication.

Yet Frances was best known at first as an antislavery lecturer. She was very active and outspoken about equal rights for blacks and women. After her marriage to Fenton Harper in 1860, Frances retired from public life. Four years later, when her husband died, she resumed traveling throughout the South speaking to the newly freed men and women.

Frances was such a appealing and eloquent speaker, many people thought that she could not possibly be a black woman. Some said she was a man. Others thought that perhaps she was painted to look black. Such ridiculous ideas served only to illustrate the very point Frances was trying to make: that African Americans and women were equal to white men in every respect.

Frances was very popular and successful as a poet and a lecturer, but she was also a political activist and a novelist. Her one and only novel, *Iola Leroy*, was published in Philadelphia in 1892 when she was 67 years old. The book, which tells of black life during the Civil War and after, was praised by white critics at that time and enjoyed some success. After a third printing in 1895, the book fell into oblivion. It was reprinted again 80 years later in 1971, and again in the 1980s.

Ignored by many scholars of African-American literature over the years, *Iola Leroy*'s place in history has now been assured by black feminists who hold Frances Harper in high esteem as an African-American woman, writer, and intellectual.

Edmonia Lewis

Premier Woman Sculptor
1843–1900(?)
Birthplace: Albany, New York

I don't want you to praise me. . . Some praise me because I am a colored girl, and I don't want that kind of praise. I had rather you would point out my defects, for that will teach me something.

E dmonia Lewis was such a talented sculptor, her admirers said that she seemed to make stones "talk." Each of her sculptures tells a story. One of her most famous, *Forever Free*, is a study of a black man greeting freedom. Wearing the broken chains of slavery, one of his hands is clenched in a fist, the other protects his wife. The sculpture captures the two strong feelings that many black people felt when they were declared free of slavery: joy in their freedom and fear that it would be taken away.

Edmonia also created busts of famous people who fought to end slavery. Her likenesses of John Brown, Charles Sumner, Col. Robert Gould Shaw, and William Story truly captured the spirit that made these men strong fighters for justice.

Edmonia's father was an African and her mother was a Native American of the Chippewa tribe. At her mother's request, Edmonia—whose Indian name meant Wildfire—lived with the Chippewa for three years. Then her brother prompted her to get a formal education. With his help, she attended school at Oberlin. After leaving Oberlin, she moved to Boston and further developed her artistic talent. Later she went to Rome, Italy, where she set up a studio and studied what is called the neoclassical style of sculpture.

Edmonia not only expressed her antislavery beliefs in her artwork, but in her actions as well. She was involved in the "Underground Railroad" that made it possible for slaves to escape to the North. She also helped organize support for one of the first black regiments that fought in the Civil War.

As one of America's first widely recognized African-American artists, Edmonia was also the first black woman to be acknowledged as a sculptor. A few of her better known works include *Hagar in the Wilderness*, *The Marriage of Hiawatha* (in tribute to her mother), and *The Death of Cleopatra*.

Augusta Savage

Fighter for Black Artists
1900–1962
Birthplace: Green Cove, Florida

If I can inspire one of these youngsters to develop the talent I know they possess, then my monument will be in their work.

At the age of six, when Augusta first started modeling clay figures, her Methodist minister father strongly objected. But Augusta had a passion and talent for sculpting that her father could not suppress.

While still a high school student herself, Augusta was allowed to teach the other students clay modeling. She enjoyed teaching, but her desire to learn more about art took her to New York's Cooper Union. There she became one of the first women to study sculpture. However, because she was so poor, Augusta almost had to drop out of school. Her instructors were so impressed with her talent, they convinced the school's board to give her financial support.

At about the same time, the New York Public Library hired Augusta to do a sculpture of W.E.B. Du Bois. Augusta's bust of the famous black leader is still considered to be the finest rendering of Du Bois in existence. Commissions for other sculptures followed, and the young artist was on her way to establishing a career in fine arts.

In 1930, Augusta won a scholarship that allowed her to study in France. When she returned to Harlem, she opened her own school, the Savage School of Arts and Crafts, where she taught young people free of charge. It was there that such African-American artists as William Artis, Norman Lewis, and Ernest Crichlow first learned their crafts.

In 1938, Augusta was commissioned to do a sculpture for the 1939–40 New York World's Fair. The result, entitled *Lift Every Voice and Sing*, based on the James Weldon Johnson poem, featured a group of singers arranged in a harp shape. It symbolized the strong musical contributions African Americans made to this country, and became Augusta's most famous work. Because funds could not be found to have the sculpture cast in bronze, it was destroyed after the World's Fair closed, but Augusta Savage's legacy lives on in the work of her many students—just as she had hoped.

Zora Neale Hurston

Protector of Black Folklore
1903–1960
Birthplace: Eatonville, Florida

Here is peace. She pulled in her horizon like a giant fish-net. Pulled it around the waist of the world and draped it over her shoulder. So much of life in its meshes. She called in her soul to come and see!

—from *Their Eyes Were Watching God*

Zora was a bright little girl with a mischievous spirit. Her father warned that her curiosity would get her in trouble, that "the white folks wouldn't stand for it." But her mother told her to "jump at the sun," and that is just what Zora did.

Born and raised in Eatonville, a self-governing black town in Florida, Zora loved to listen to stories on the back porch of the general store where people in her town gathered. It was there that she developed a love for language and folktales.

Zora studied anthropology at Barnard College. Anthropology is the study of human beings, and this influenced Zora as she collected folktales from all over the South and parts of the Caribbean. The books she wrote that resulted from her studies and travels—such as *Their Eyes Were Watching God*—not only celebrated the lives of black people, but documented them as well. Writers to this day admire her unique gift of storytelling, which captures everyday African-American life in its wonderful style.

Zora was a major figure in the Harlem Renaissance—that period in history in the 1920s and 1930s when the work of African-American writers and artists was widely recognized. But she never received the fame and support that was enjoyed by writers such as Langston Hughes and Richard Wright. Some people believe that Zora, although a talented writer, was overlooked because she was a woman.

On January 28, 1960, Zora died poor and unknown. But today a new generation has discovered her work. Thanks to the interest of such contemporary writers as Alice Walker, many of Zora's books have been reprinted and several books have been written about her. Her life and work are also being celebrated in stage plays around the country. Zora is now beginning to receive the recognition she so richly deserved.

Margaret Walker

Poet, Author, Master Teacher
1915–
Birthplace: Birmingham, Alabama

[T]he most wonderful thing, next to a human being, [is] a book.

I t was no surprise that Margaret Walker became a writer. Her mother was a teacher who constantly read stories and poems to her four children. Her father was a minister who spoke five languages. Because of her parents' work and interests, Margaret not only grew up with books, she met many of the African-American poets and writers of the time, including Langston Hughes and Richard Wright.

From her maternal grandmother, young Margaret would hear stories about her great-grandmother who was enslaved. Margaret was very moved by the stories of her ancestors' struggles, and she promised her grandmother that she would one day write her great-grandmother's story.

A gifted child, Margaret entered college at age 15. When she was 22 years old, she wrote a poem called, "For My People," which called for strength and pride among black people. The poem became famous and won her the Yale Younger Poets Competition in 1942.

Margaret later became a professor of English and African-American literature and history at Jackson State University in Mississippi. Her students loved the way she helped them understand literature by explaining the lives of the authors. In the 1960s, Margaret established the Institute for the Study of Black Life and Culture at Jackson State, the first of its kind in the South. She accomplished all of these things while raising her family, studying for advanced degrees, and writing her books.

In 1966, Margaret kept her promise to her grandmother by completing her novel, *Jubilee*, based on the stories of her great-grandmother's life. The 20 years Margaret spent researching the book was worth it: *Jubilee* became one of the most famous books ever written by a black woman.

In 1979, after 40 years, Margaret Walker retired from teaching to devote her energies to writing full-time. In 1988, her biography of her friend, *Richard Wright: Daemonic Genius*, was published.

Gwendolyn Brooks

Bard of Bronzeville
1917–
Birthplace: Topeka, Kansas

My aim . . . is to write poems that will somehow successfully "call". . .all black people. . . . I wish to reach black people in pulpits, black people in mines, on farms, on thrones.

Gwendolyn knew at a very early age that she wanted to be a poet. By the time she was 11 years old she had published her first four poems. While encouragement from her parents and from the famous African-American writer James Weldon Johnson helped to fire her enthusiasm, incidents that occurred in the lives of black people served as inspiration. For example, when 14-year-old Emmett Till was murdered in Mississippi because he allegedly whistled at a white woman, Gwendolyn couldn't rest until she had written poems about that tragic event. "A Bronzeville Mother Loiters in Mississippi..." and "The Last Quatrain of Emmett Till" were the results.

Gwendolyn attended college in Chicago and also taught there. But her dedication to writing never wavered. In 1950, after years of perfecting her craft, Gwendolyn, at the age of 33, won the Pulitzer Prize for her second volume of poems, *Annie Allen*. She was the first African American to ever win that prestigious award.

Like the poems in *Annie Allen*, which express the joy and pain of black urban life, Gwendolyn's later work shows an intense concern for racial issues. *In the Mecca*, published in 1968, is a collection of poems that express her commitment to the political and cultural self-awareness of her people.

This commitment was also demonstrated when she left Harper & Row, a white publisher, in order to be published by Dudley Randall's Broadside Press. *Riot* and her autobiography, *Report from Part One*, are some of her works published by Broadside. Written during the 1960s' civil rights movement, these collections encourage black people to work together to bring about their real freedom.

Among the many awards Gwendolyn Brooks has received are the American Academy of Arts and Letters award for creative writing (1946); Guggenheim Fellowships (1946, 1947); the Anisfield-Wolf Award for *In the Mecca* (1968); Poet Laureate of Illinois in 1968; and the Black Academy of Arts and Letters Award in 1971.

Alice Childress

Playwright and Novelist
1920–
Birthplace: Charleston, South Carolina

My young years were very old in feeling. I was shut out of so much for so long. [I] soon began to embrace the low-profile as a way of life, which helped me to develop as a writer. Quiet living is restful when one's writing is labeled "controversial."

Writer Alice Childress actually began her career as an actress. Her stage debut was in 1940 in a play called *On Strivers Row*. For 11 years she studied and worked as an actress and director with the American Negro Theatre in New York City. Then, in 1952, Alice's play *Gold Through the Trees* became the first play by an African-American woman ever to be professionally produced on the American stage. Alice's successful career as a playwright began.

Unafraid of criticism, Alice writes with honesty about racism and other controversial subjects. Through her characters she comments on the pain and injustice that can be found throughout American society. Her play *Trouble in Mind*, for example, focuses on the plight of African-American actors who are often expected to play stereotyped roles. Her novel, *A Hero Ain't Nothin' but a Sandwich*, is about teenage heroin addiction.

Widely acclaimed for its frank treatment of drug addiction, *A Hero Ain't Nothin' but a Sandwich* was made into a movie in 1977 starring Cicely Tyson. The book was named "One of the Outstanding Books of the Year" by *The New York Times Book Review* in 1973 and a Best Young Adult Books in 1975 by the American Library Association.

Alice's novel *Rainbow Jordan*, a work she wrote for children, also received many awards. It was named one of the Best Books by the *School Library Journal* and won a Coretta Scott King Honor Award.

A versatile writer, Alice has displayed her talent in several genres. Her plays have received honors as well: *Trouble in Mind* won a "Best Play" Obie Award, and *Wedding Band* was performed on ABC-TV. In all of her work, her characters display strength and insight, qualities that have helped her win respect and praise.

Alice Childress is a writer who is not afraid to write the truth, no matter how harsh the truth might be.

Maya Angelou

Renaissance Woman
1928–
Birthplace: St. Louis, Missouri

I weep a lot. I thank God I laugh a lot, too.
The main thing in one's own private world is
to try to laugh as much as you cry.

Maya Angelou, who was born Marguerite Johnson, is an author, poet, songwriter, dancer, actor, director, and producer. She's been nominated for a Tony award for her acting, a Pulitzer Prize for her poetry, and a National Book Award for her autobiography, *I Know Why the Caged Bird Sings.*

Yet this remarkable artist suffered a difficult and unhappy childhood. When she was eight years old, she was raped by one of her mother's friends. The man was later killed by a lynch mob. Maya was so traumatized, she did not speak for five years.

With the love and support of her grandmother and her brother, Bailey, Maya slowly overcame her fear and handicap. At the same time, she sought to express herself in other ways. Although a voracious reader, Maya also studied modern dance. She danced and acted professionally for 16 years, traveling around the world. She also started writing magazine articles for African publications, and songs for blues singer B. B. King. Upon her return to the United States, she wrote, produced, and appeared in many shows for television and stage.

Maya is best known for her book *I Know Why the Caged Bird Sings,* in which she describes being black and female in the South during the Depression. The book was made into a television movie and was the first of a five-part series of autobiographical books, which includes *Just Give Me a Cool Drink of Water 'Fore I Diie* and *Gather Together in My Name.* The idea for her autobiography came during a dinner conversation with some of her friends, including the famous African-American novelist, James Baldwin.

Among Maya's considerable accomplishments is the fact that she was the first black woman director in Hollywood. Ever vigilant of and sensitive to the struggles of African Americans, Maya has found some peace in what she calls her second home in Ghana, West Africa. Since 1981 she has taught at Wake Forest University where she was appointed to a lifetime position as the first Reynolds Professor of American Studies.

Lorraine Hansberry

Young, Gifted, and Black
1930–1965
Birthplace: Chicago, Illinois

I care. I admit it. I care about it all. It takes too much energy not to care!

—from *To Be Young, Gifted and Black*, Act II

When Lorraine Hansberry was a girl, her family moved to a white neighborhood. This was during a time when black and white people usually lived in separate parts of town. Many of the neighbors were angry that the Hansberry family had moved into their white area. When Lorraine walked to school, some of them called her names and made fun of her. She was often very frightened during her childhood, and she never forgot those experiences.

Lorraine went on to study drama and stage design at the University of Wisconsin, and painting at the Art Institute of Chicago. Remembering how hard her family fought back against discrimination, she wrote a play to tell the world how she felt. *A Raisin in the Sun* is about an African American who wants to move into a white neighborhood. The play illustrates the love, pride, and strength that hold many black families together. It was the first play written by an African-American woman to be produced in New York on Broadway, and it became Lorraine's most famous work.

The 1959 Broadway production was produced, directed, and acted by African Americans—an occurence that was, and is, very rare. Sidney Poitier, Glynn Turman, Ivan Dixon, and Ruby Dee were featured in the cast. *A Raisin in the Sun* became the longest running play by a black author up to that time and won the New York Drama Critics Circle Award. It was later produced as a musical called *Raisin*, which won a 1974 Tony Award.

Lorraine also wrote poetry, articles, and a book—*To Be Young, Gifted and Black*—which was also produced as a play. She died of cancer shortly after her second play, *The Sign in Sidney Brustein's Window*, opened on Broadway. She was only 34 years old, but she will always be remembered as one of America's finest playwrights.

Toni Morrison

Prize-Winning Novelist
1931–
Birthplace: Lorraine, Ohio

*I really think the range of emotions and
perceptions I have had access to as a black
person and a female person are greater than
those of people who are neither. . . . My world
did not shrink because I was a black female
writer. It just got bigger.*

T oni Morrison (born Chloe Anthony Wofford) is a painter, and her books are her canvases. They are vivid pictures of black American life painted in words that are true to the language of black people. Her books portray experiences of African-American women that were never before described, making Toni Morrison not simply a good writer but a great one.

In 1953, Toni graduated from Howard University in Washington, D.C. Two years later, she received a master's degree from Cornell University. She then returned to Howard to teach and to write. In 1965, she worked as a senior editor at Random House, a publishing company in New York City. When she realized that white editors were not giving the works of black writers any serious consideration for publication, she did not rest until she had changed that situation. Under her direction, such African-American authors as Toni Cade Bambara, Gayl Jones, Angela Davis, and Muhammed Ali were published by Random House.

One of Toni's projects at Random House was *The Black Book*, an anthology about the history of black America. While preparing *The Black Book* for publication, Toni discovered the tragically true story of a runaway slave who, upon being recaptured, murdered her baby so the child would not spend a lifetime in slavery. That story formed the nucleus of Toni's fifth novel, *Beloved*, which won the Pulitzer Prize for Literature in 1988. Toni has written four other novels: *Song of Solomon*, *The Bluest Eye*, *Sula*, and *Tar Baby*. All of her books have been critically acclaimed.

Throughout her childhood Toni heard many tales from her parents and her grandmother— many contained supernatural elements. Toni weaves those childhood stories into her novels, adding a mysterious quality to her works.

Toni believes there is power and grace in the language of black people. She has proven her ability to let readers feel those qualities as she draws them into the worlds of her novels.

Alice Walker

Womanist Writer
1944–
Birthplace: Eatonton, Georgia

The black woman is one of America's greatest heroes.

Alice Malsenior Walker was a bright outgoing child, the youngest of eight children. Her father, who was "wonderful at math [but] a terrible farmer," was a sharecropper. Her mother helped her father in the fields and worked as a maid. Even though her family was poor, they were very creative. Both of her parents were strong storytellers, and Alice remembers her mother working hard to make the shacks that they lived in look beautiful.

Yet it took a tragic accident for Alice to discover her own talents. At age eight, she was wounded in the eye by a shot from a BB gun that one of her brothers had fired. Without a car, the family had to wait a week to take her to the doctor. By that time, Alice was permanently blind in that eye. Self-conscious about her disfigurement, Alice found comfort in reading and writing poetry. She became so good at her craft that she was awarded several fellowships and had many volumes of her poetry published.

Alice first attended Spelman College and then went on to Sarah Lawrence. She continued to write all the while. After graduation, she worked in New York City's Welfare Department — a job that she "couldn't stand"—and worked on her writing at night.

In 1970, Alice Walker published her first novel, *The Third Life of Grange Copeland*, which looks at the effects of racism and sexism on three generations of a sharecropping family. Another novel and two collections of short stories followed. Then Alice wrote her most famous work, *The Color Purple*, for which she won the American Book Award and the Pulitzer Prize. *The Color Purple* was also made into a movie of the same name that was nominated for 11 Academy Awards.

Alice Walker is a writer deeply concerned about women's issues. She is also extremely concerned about the welfare and "wholeness" of her people and of all people. As such, Alice Walker is more than a feminist writer. She is, by her own definition, a "womanist" writer. *Possessing the Secret of Joy* and *The Temple of My Familiar* are two of her most recent works.

Lorna Simpson

Innovative Photographer
1960–
Birthplace: Brooklyn, New York

The viewer wants so much to see a face, to read "the look in the eyes," or the expression on the mouth. . . .

As a child, Lorna excelled in drawing and painting. She attended New York City's High School of Art and Design, went on to college at the School of Visual Arts, and then to graduate school at the University of California, San Diego.

Early in her career, Lorna Simpson would take documentary photographs of street scenes of New York, Africa, and Europe. They showed ordinary people doing ordinary things. But when these works were exhibited, Lorna was unhappy with the way people made assumptions about the meanings of her photographs.

Most artists do not allow the reactions of the audience to determine the way they paint, sculpt, or photograph. But this was very important to Lorna. She wanted the people who saw her photographs to understand them as she did. To solve the problem, Lorna decided that she would no longer allow the viewer to see the faces of her subjects.

Lorna began photographing models in a studio. From these photos, she selected details—such as close up views of hair, the back, or arms—for the audience to see. She then described the photograph with words or a brief phrase that she attached to the photo. In this way, she is able to explain what *she* sees in the picture.

Most of Lorna's subjects are black women. Through her pictures, Lorna is able to make the viewer think about the way in which women—particularly black women—are classified and analyzed.

In 1990, at age 30, Lorna became the first black woman whose work was exhibited in the Venice Biennale, the most important international art exhibition in the world. That same year, she was also the first black woman to be given a solo exhibition in the Painting and Sculpture department of the Museum of Modern Art in New York City. With this success, Lorna Simpson has entered the ranks of such prominent African-American photographers as Gordon Parks and James VanDerZee.

Performing Artists

BEARING WITNESS THROUGH SELF-EXPRESSION

Judith Jamison performs *Cry.*

I am a singer, not a politician,
but . . . every song I sing
becomes a statement that echoes the hopes
and aspirations of my people.

—Miriam Makeba

Hattie McDaniel

First Black Academy-Award Winner
1898–1952
Birthplace: Wichita, Kansas

It's much better to play a maid than to be one.

Hattie McDaniel was a spirited child with a great sense of humor. She liked play-acting and being the center of attention—not an easy thing to achieve with 12 brothers and sisters! Hattie never stopped performing. As a teenager, she sang as an amateur on a radio show. Later she worked as a professional vaudeville performer. During the 1930s, she even starred in a radio show as "Hi-Hat Hattie."

As an adult, Hattie was a large lady with smooth, chocolate-colored skin, a big round face, expressive eyes, a bright smile, and a booming voice. By the time she was 33, Hattie had made her way to Hollywood. To support herself, she took work as a maid and cleaning woman. Gradually, she started to get movie roles, but she always had to play a maid.

There were many black servant roles in films in those days. Usually, these parts called for the characters to simply do their duties, seldom talk, always smile, and to be obedient. Of course, such portrayals reflected the inferior status that white people gave to black people. Most actors who played servants were easy to forget once the scene was over.

But Hattie played her servant roles in a different way. She used her spirited personality and talent for comedy to make the maids she played unforgettable. She always made them wise, and often made them outspoken. While pretending to be the perfect servant, she would put her employers in their place without acting subservient. Hattie's style was so respected by directors, that she appeared in over 20 films in the 1930s.

In 1939, Hattie used all of those personality traits in a role as a maid in the famous film, *Gone With the Wind*. The film became a classic, and for her part in it Hattie McDaniel won the 1940 Academy Award for Best Supporting Actress. She became the first black actor or actress to win an Oscar.

Marian Anderson

A Voice Loved Around the World
1902–1993
Birthplace: Philadelphia, Pennsylvania

I don't feel that I opened a door . . . . I think that those who came after me deserve a great deal of credit for what they have achieved. I don't feel that I am responsible for any of it, because if they didn't have it in them, they wouldn't be able to get it out.

Marian Anderson always loved to sing, so when she was six, she joined her church choir. Church members were so impressed by the child's natural talent, they set up a trust fund to help pay for her musical training.

Marian began studying formally with a renowned voice teacher when she was 19. Later, she entered and won a major competition that gave her the chance of performing with the New York Philharmonic as a concert singer. She then won a Rosenwald Fellowship and made her European debut in Berlin in 1930. For the next five years, Marian toured Europe, establishing herself as one of the world's finest contraltos. Upon her return to the United States, Marian was triumphant in her recitals at New York City's Town Hall and Carnegie Hall. A *New York Times* reviewer described her performance as "music making that probed too deep for words."

In spite of her fame, Marian was denied many opportunities back home in America because she was African American. In 1939, the Daughters of the American Revolution refused to let her perform at Constitution Hall in Washington, D.C. Eleanor Roosevelt, President Franklin D. Roosevelt's wife and a member of the organization, resigned in protest. She then arranged for Marian to sing on the steps of the Lincoln Memorial. On Easter morning, 1939, more than 75,000 people heard this talented woman in concert. In 1942, a Marian Anderson Award for young singers was established.

Never letting discrimination stop her, Marian made headlines when she became the first African American to sing a leading role at the Metropolitan Opera in New York City. During her brilliant career, she sang in countries all over the world, and millions of her records have been sold. In 1958, President Dwight D. Eisenhower appointed her a delegate to the United Nations. Marian retired in 1965.

In 1978, she was presented the first John F. Kennedy Center Honor, one of five people to receive the prestigious award that year.

Mary Lou Williams

The First Lady of Jazz
1910–1981
Birthplace: Atlanta, Georgia

*I think that anyone with ears can identify me
without any difficulty!*

Mary (born Mary Elfrieda Winn) and most of her seven brothers and sisters were
musically talented. As a young child, Mary would sit on her mother's lap while she
played the organ. Soon Mary was able to pick out ragtime tunes on the organ herself.

Mary became so good on the keyboard that by the time she was 16, she was leading her
own jazz band. She soon developed a reputation as a gifted composer and arranger, and was
hired to write musical arrangements for many famous band leaders such as Louis Armstrong,
Tommy Dorsey, Duke Ellington, and Benny Goodman. With these bands and others, Mary
Lou traveled and performed all over the world.

Mary Lou's style of piano playing reflected the whole history of jazz: stride, boogie woogie,
and bebop. She did not have a gentle, dainty way of playing, either. When Mary played, she
gave those keys a powerful, driving workout!

In addition to being generous with her musical talents, Mary Lou was generous of spirit.
She dedicated her life to helping fellow musicians in need. Many jazz musicians—including
trumpeter Dizzy Gillespie, saxophonist Charlie Parker, and pianist Thelonius Monk—often
met at Mary Lou's home to relax, discuss the music scene, encourage each other, and work
on their craft.

Later, Mary Lou established the Bel Canto Foundation to help musicians who had become
involved with alcohol or drugs. In 1977, she also began teaching jazz history and improvi-
sation full-time at Duke University in North Carolina.

Mary Lou Williams died of cancer in 1981. But before her death, she established another
foundation—the Mary Lou Williams Foundation. She left her entire estate to this foundation
to help gifted young musicians study music with jazz professionals. Along with her music, this
was Mary Lou's gift to future generations of jazz lovers.

Katherine Dunham

Pioneer of Black Dance
1910–
Birthplace: Joliet, Illinois

In knowing how to overcome little things, a centimeter at a time, gradually, when bigger things come, you're prepared. You're not taken by surprise, you're not even angry or upset. It just rouses your spirit to do more.

Katherine Dunham is a dancer, choreographer, and anthropologist who has used her many talents to make an important gift to the world. But as a child growing up in Illinois, Katherine didn't know what that gift would be. She knew she was different, that she didn't seem to fit in anywhere. It wasn't until her older brother Albert brought her into his theater group in Chicago that Katherine found her place in dance theater.

When Katherine was a college student, she won a scholarship to study anthropology in Haiti. While she was there, she studied Haitian dances. Katherine realized how important these dances were and believed that they could teach people many things about black history and culture. She knew these dances should be shared with the rest of world. So when she returned to the United States, she brought the dances with her. She also documented her findings in a book, *Dances of Haiti*, which has been reprinted in several languages.

Katherine formed an all-black dance company that became internationally famous. But the company faced many problems at home. Because the troupe was black, hotels would often not admit them. And they often had to practice in small, cramped rooms. At first Katherine's work was more respected overseas than in the United States. Since 1947, the company has performed in nearly 60 countries.

Through her work with her company, and in musicals like *Cabin in the Sky* and *Stormy Weather*, Katherine introduced African and Caribbean rhythms and movements to Americans. Yet it wasn't until much later in her life that she was recognized for her contributions. In January 1979, Katherine was presented the prestigious Albert Schweitzer Music Award at Carnegie Hall in New York City. In December 1983, Katherine received a Kennedy Center Honor—the nation's highest award for an artist, for her work as a dancer, choreographer, and anthropologist. In 1986, she received the Scripps American Dance Festival Award. All of these honors were well deserved and long overdue.

Mahalia Jackson

The World's Greatest Gospel Singer
1911–1972
Birthplace: New Orleans, Louisiana

It has meant so much to me that a great part of the brave fight for freedom down South is now coming from inside the church and from the hymns and gospel songs the people are singing.

T he "little girl with the big voice" started singing in her Sunday school choir before she was five years old. By the time she left New Orleans for Chicago in 1927, Mahalia Jackson, at age 16, had already sung in church many of the songs that would later make her famous.

Mahalia's childhood dreams were of becoming a nurse, not a singer. She went to Chicago to attend nursing school, but life there wasn't easy. Working as a washerwoman, she barely had enough money for room and board. Tuition for nursing school was out of the question.

It was a depressing time for Mahalia, but her church activities helped her through it. Just as her church in New Orleans had been the center of her life, so too was her church in Chicago—the Greater Salem Baptist Church. There Mahalia became involved with a gospel singing group formed by the minister's sons. Mahalia was so good, she soon began performing and touring alone.

The deep, rich quality of Mahalia's voice—a quality that moved to tears almost everyone who heard her sing—attracted many people. This included the managers of a recording studio in Chicago, who paid Mahalia $25 for her first song in 1934. That year was the fifth year of the Great Depression, a time when most people had very little money, so $25 was a fortune to Mahalia.

In 1946, Mahalia recorded "Move on Up a Little Higher," the song that made her famous and earned her a real fortune—$100,000—in profits. Soon she was appearing in concerts at home and abroad.

Actively involved in the struggle against racial injustice, Mahalia met Reverend Martin Luther King, Jr. and Reverend Ralph Abernathy who asked her to sing at a civil rights rally in Montgomery, Alabama, in 1955. This was the beginning of a close association with Dr. King and the civil rights movement, and, until her death, Mahalia donated her time, money, and talent to the struggle for a better America.

Lena Horne

The Lady and Her Music
1917–
Birthplace: Brooklyn, New York

*I was always battling the system to try to get
to be with my people. Finally, I wouldn't work
for places that kept us out. I couldn't get a
place to live, so I fought for housing. The mere
fact of living had to be fought, because I was
black and I never lost sight of that.*

At age two, Lena Horne made her public debut when a 1919 issue of the NAACP's *Crisis* magazine published a picture of their youngest member. Up until age 15, she accompanied her grandmother to meetings held by such civil rights organizations as the Urban League and the NAACP.

But it was when Lena joined the chorus line of Harlem's famous Cotton Club at age 16 that the course of her legendary life was set. She worked at the Cotton Club for two years, where she received low pay but achieved high visibility. She soon came to the attention of a producer who offered her a part in a Broadway show. During the show's short run another producer, Noble Sissle, noticed Lena and hired her to sing with his all-black band. While touring with the band, Lena caught the eye of a Metro-Goldwyn-Meyer (MGM) talent scout who signed her to work for the powerful studio.

With her appearances in *The Duke Is Tops* (her first film), and such 1940s' MGM classics as *Cabin in the Sky* and *Stormy Weather*, Lena became the first black woman in American films to be glamorized. She insisted that she would not play stereotypical roles—such as maids— that were being offered to black actresses at that time, and MGM agreed.

Like Hattie McDaniel, Lena also encountered racism in Hollywood (her film scenes were often cut so that they would not offend white audiences), but her inner strength helped her to face unjust and unpleasant situations. Throughout her career she has used her talent and success to fight for civil rights. She has sung at many rallies and fundraisers, continues to work with the NAACP and other civil rights organizations, and has even cancelled engagements in protest over unjust treatment of African Americans.

From May 1981 to June 1982, Lena appeared in a one-person show on Broadway entitled *Lena Horne: The Lady and Her Music.* For the longest-running one-woman show in the history of Broadway, Lena received a Tony Award, a Drama Desk Award, a special citation from the New York Drama Critics Circle, and the Handel Medallion, New York's highest cultural award.

Ella Fitzgerald

First Lady of Song
1918–
Birthplace: Newport News, Virginia

I just like music . . . period. I always try to picture something in every kind of music. To me it's a story.

As a young child, Ella Fitzgerald lost both of her parents. She was raised in an orphanage in Yonkers, New York. When Ella was 15 she entered an amateur contest at New York's Apollo Theater. She intended to sing and dance that night, but she was so nervous, she found that she couldn't dance, so she just sang a song instead. Little did she know that her performance that evening would change her life. Chick Webb, a famous jazz drummer and band leader, was in the audience. He was looking for a new singer for his band, and when he heard Ella, he knew she was the one. He hired her on the spot.

Chick Webb and his wife took her into their home where he directed and guided Ella in singing and performing. Soon she was traveling with his band,which helped propel them into national prominence. In 1938, Ella composed her most famous song with Chick Webb. "A-Tisket A-Tasket," based on an old nursery rhyme, became an immediate success, and Ella was a star.

Chick Webb died soon thereafter, but Ella continued to sing with his band for three years. Then she decided to strike out on her own. In the 50 years since her debut, Ella has traveled all over the world, displaying her incredible talent for diversity. Ella has the ability to sing any kind of song—swing, ballad, pop, calypso, Dixieland jazz—but she is best known for her "scat" singing (a style and term she practically invented). Her versatility and sensitivity to music has made her popular with fans of both jazz and popular music.

Considered the musician's musician and the singer's singer, Ella has recorded more than two thousand different songs and has more than 70 albums to her credit. She has sold over 25 million recordings during the course of her career. She has also performed with more than 40 symphony orchestras. Ella has influenced several generations of singers. As Bing Crosby once said, "Man, woman, or child, the greatest singer of them all is Ella Fitzgerald"—the First Lady of Song.

Ruby Dee

Theatrical Pioneer
1923–
Birthplace: Cleveland, Ohio

I like the idea of people striving to be better and to make the world better. . . . That's what being young is all about. You have the courage and the daring to think that you can make a difference.

Ruby Ann Wallace changed her name to Ruby Dee when she started acting in the 1940s. She studied and perfected her craft with other young African-American actors like Sidney Poitier and Ossie Davis (whom Ruby later married) at Harlem's American Negro Theater. She made her stage debut in a play called *South Pacific*.

Even though there were very few good movie roles for black actors at that time, Ruby Dee played several notable film parts. In the 1950s, she appeared in movies like *Edge of the City*, with Sidney Poitier, and *A Raisin in the Sun*, based on the play by Lorraine Hansberry. Later Ruby frequently worked in television in such movies as "I Know Why the Caged Bird Sings," based on Maya Angelou's famous autobiography, and "Roots: The Next Generation." On stage Ruby became the first black actress to play major parts at the American Shakespeare Festival. As a result of her many and diverse performances, she has become one of America's most recognized black actresses. She was recently seen in films by director Spike Lee, *Do the Right Thing* and *Jungle Fever*.

Ruby has also worked on many projects with her husband, Ossie Davis. He is not only an actor but a writer and television and film director as well. Ossie Davis wrote the play *Purlie Victorious*, and Ruby starred in its original production. Together they hosted the television series "With Ossie and Ruby" in 1981.

Ruby is also a writer, a storyteller, and a poet. Recently she has published a collection of her poetry called *My One Last Nerve*, and a children's book, *Two Ways to Count to Ten*.

African-American actresses have always found it difficult to make a living because there are very few good roles written for them. But Ruby never gave up. She worked hard to sharpen her skills as an actor, a writer, a wife, and a mother, and she applied them with care and determination to fight the many forms of discrimination she encountered in her life.

Sarah Vaughan

"The Divine One"
1924–1990
Birthplace: Newark, New Jersey

I just sing. I don't know what I sound like or who I sound like. I don't know what kind of singer I am. I just open my mouth and sing.

L ike many African-American singers, Sarah Vaughan's musical beginnings can be found in the church, where she played piano and organ, and sang in the choir. When she was 18 years old, Sarah entered an amateur talent contest at the famous Apollo Theater in New York City just for fun. She won and her prize was a week performing at the theater. Ella Fitzgerald was the star performer during that week, and Sarah felt so honored to be able to sing on the same bill as Ella. Two weeks later, Sarah was hired as a singer by the famous jazz pianist Earl "Fatha" Hines, and that was the start of her professional singing career.

Teenager Sarah quickly learned the ropes of the music business from the more seasoned musicians who worked with her in Earl Hines and Billy Eckstine's bands. They called her "sassy" because her singing style and performing skills were so unique.

It has been said that Sarah was the first real jazz singer with the vocal range equal to that of an opera singer. In fact, opera singer Leontyne Price was the performer whose voice Sarah admired most. However, Sarah listened to horn players more than singers to develop her style. As a result, she could do many amazing things with her voice. She recorded both jazz and popular songs—always adding special little touches that would make each song an original. Sarah especially enjoyed good lyrics. She would often play with the words, stretching one syllable into several, or making her voice go from high to low with lightening speed.

Although Sarah loved her audiences and their enthusiasm, she hated when they clapped in time to the music. Whenever her audience would start clapping, sassy Sarah would change the rhythm of her singing just enough to confuse them, until they stopped clapping!

Sarah became a major force on the jazz scene. She loved show business, and she continued to perform until she died of lung cancer in Beverly Hills, California, in 1990.

Leontyne Price

Diva
1927–
Birthplace: Laurel, Mississippi

Accomplishments have no color.

When Leontyne was about six years old, she received a toy piano for Christmas. The attention she got when she played it made her feel wonderful, so she decided then that she was going to be a performer when she grew up.

Leontyne was born Mary Leontyne Price. Her mother was a midwife. Leontyne was very proud of her, because her mother delivered more babies than any midwife in Jones County, Mississippi. Leontyne's mother was also her greatest inspiration.

One day Leontyne's mother took her to see a concert given by the famous African-American singer, Marian Anderson. When Leontyne saw Marian Anderson emerge onto the stage in her beautiful white dress, she immediately knew that she, too, would be on stage one day.

When Leontyne was 22 years old, she earned a scholarship to the Julliard School of Music in New York City. Three years later, she was cast in the all-black Broadway play, *Four Saints in Three Acts*. Her clear, strong soprano voice was so impressive that she was then chosen to sing the part of Bess in the famous all-black opera by George Gershwin called *Porgy and Bess*. Leontyne's performance in *Porgy and Bess* soon brought her talents to the attention of the world of traditional European opera. Leontyne learned to sing many parts written in Italian, Spanish, and German. Her first Grand Opera performance of Verdi's *Aïda* in 1957 could not be equaled.

On January 27, 1961, Leontyne made her debut at the Metropolitan Opera in *Il Trovatore*. When she finished singing, she received a 42-minute ovation from the audience. Critics have called Leontyne's soprano voice one of the "great operatic voices of the age."

When the Metropolitan Opera moved to its new home in New York City's Lincoln Center in 1966, Leontyne opened the season as Cleopatra in *Antony and Cleopatra*, an opera written especially for her. Her career has continued to climb upward ever since. She has appeared in operas all over the world, has recorded numerous records, and has received many awards, including 18 Grammy Awards. In 1990, Leontyne's children's book *Aïda* won the Coretta Scott King Award for excellence.

Miriam Makeba

Empress of African Song
1932–
Birthplace: Johannesburg, South Africa

[I]n a sad world where so many are victims, I can take pride that I am also a fighter. My life, my career, every song I sing and every appearance I make, are bound up with the plight of my people.

Miriam Makeba, a member of the Xhosa people, was born in a township outside of Johannesburg, South Africa. Music was always an important part of her life, and she discovered at a young age that she had an exceptional singing voice. Miriam's voice was so beautiful that she earned a place in her school's senior chorus before she entered the junior class.

In 1952, when Miriam was 20, *The Bantu World*, an important black South African newspaper, published the first review of her singing career. The reviewer wrote that Miriam sang like a nightingale. Since then audiences throughout the world have heard "the nightingale" sing about her land, her people, and her dream for a free South Africa.

Like all black South Africans, Miriam lived under the oppressive conditions of apartheid. Apartheid is the unjust system of government that forces black South Africans to live, work, and receive education apart from white South Africans. But despite the harsh apartheid laws, Miriam and other singers toured her country giving concerts. Often they were arrested and put in jail for no good reason.

In 1956, Miriam sang in a documentary film about the life of a black man in South Africa. *Come Back Africa* won international acclaim and brought Miriam into a world outside of South Africa. People invited her to give concerts in Europe and the United States. "The Click Song," sung in Xhosa (a language that has many clicking sounds), and "Pata Pata" are two of her most popular songs.

Miriam has condemned apartheid during all of her concerts and during the speeches she has made at the United Nations. Because she was critical of its racist policies, the South African government exiled Miriam and banned her records from South Africa. But Miriam's fame grew as a singer and as a spokesperson against apartheid. Several African countries awarded her honorary citizenships, and she lived for many years in Guinea, a West African nation. She has recently been allowed to return home to South Africa.

Nina Simone

High Priestess of Soul
1935–
Birthplace: Tryon, North Carolina

Miss Simone . . . stirs her listeners' emotions more skillfully . . . than any other popular singer.

—Music critic John S. Wilson, 1960s

Nina (born Eunice Kathleen Waymon) was interested in music from the time she was a child. But at first she did not express her talent by singing. She began playing piano by ear when she was three years old. When Eunice was seven, a white woman for whom her mother worked agreed to pay for her piano lessons. In high school, Eunice was active in the student council and the choir, and played the piano for the glee club.

Although her family could not afford to send her to college, people who wanted to help Eunice get an education donated money. In this way, she was able to attend the prestigious Julliard School of Music in New York City. There she studied piano and theory. When the money ran out, Eunice moved back home to her family, now in Philadelphia. She helped support herself by teaching and using her husky voice to sing blues songs in Atlantic City nightclubs.

Soon, she changed her name to Nina Simone. Her first big success came in 1957 for her version of the tune "I Love You Porgy," from the play *Porgy and Bess*. At the same time, her popularity as a nightclub entertainer grew, and she made many concert tours in the United States and Europe.

In the late 1960s and 1970s, Nina began to make strong statements about civil rights and social issues through the songs she sang. Some of her songs were inspired by black poets. She put to music the words of Langston Hughes ("The Backlash Blues"), Lorraine Hansberry ("To Be Young, Gifted and Black"), and Paul Lawrence Dunbar ("Compensation"). Some songs she composed herself. "Four Women," for example, was inspired by the differences in skin color among black people.

Nina Simone's songs are not sweet, light, or pretty. They are honest, raw pieces from a woman who is not afraid to make people think about both racism and black pride— through music.

Cicely Tyson

The Consummate Actress
1938–
Birthplace: New York, New York

Role model? My mother leads the pack. When I think of the price she paid for "this life," I regard her as I do all of the other black women throughout history: miraculous. They are miracles in this human race.

After she graduated from high school, young Cicely Tyson took a job as a secretary for the Red Cross, a job that did not last long. "I'm sure God didn't intend me to sit at a typewriter," she said the day she quit, and she was right. Cicely decided to embark upon a career as a model. In 1956, she appeared on the covers of *Vogue* and *Harper's Bazaar* magazines. She also studied acting diligently and started her career on the New York stage. There she gave impressive performances that led to her break into television in the 1960s. In 1959, Cicely appeared on a CBS series, "Camera Three." She wore her hair natural and she is believed to have been the first African-American woman to do so on national television.

Although Cicely gained some attention as one of the few African-American actresses working in television at that time—and one of the few who wore an Afro hair style—it wasn't until the 1970s that her talent and artistry were widely recognized. She was nominated for an Academy Award as Best Actress in 1974 for her portrayal of the character Rebecca in the movie *Sounder*. Soon after that she won an Emmy Award for her triumphant performance as Jane Pittman in *The Autobiography of Miss Jane Pittman*, based on the novel by Ernest Gaines. Since then Cicely has appeared regularly in films, such as *A Hero Ain't Nothing But a Sandwich*, and in television movies like *Roots*, *King*, and *The Marva Collins Story*. She always portrays her characters with sensitivity and dignity.

But, like most black actors, developing such an impressive career was not easy. At one time Cicely even contemplated giving up acting because she could not find good roles to play. In the early 1970s, while other black actors were finding work in the "blaxploitation" films of that time, Cicely turned down roles that she thought were demeaning to African Americans.

The NAACP recognized Cicely's contributions to the visual arts by honoring her with seven Image Awards. Her unwavering dedication to her art and to her people have made Cicely Tyson not only a major American dramatic actress, but a major contributor to African-American culture.

Aretha Franklin

Queen of Soul
1942–
Birthplace: Memphis, Tennessee

It's not cool to be Negro or Jewish or Italian or anything else. It's just cool to be alive, to be around. You don't have to be Negro to have soul.

R -E-S-P-E-C-T. Respect. That word became very important to African Americans in the 1960s, and the song that Aretha Franklin sang became "the new Negro national anthem," earning her the undying love of her people.

Beautiful black voices were always a part of Aretha's life. Her father was a well-known preacher, and famous black singers like Dinah Washington, Mahalia Jackson, and B.B. King often visited Aretha's home. After her mother died when Aretha was ten, she immersed herself in music, singing in her father's church choir and touring with his evangelist group.

When Aretha was 12, she made her first solo record. By the time she graduated from high school, she knew she wanted to be a professional singer. At first she sang only the gospel songs she learned in her early years, but later she began to sing popular music as well.

Despite her early recognition, success did not come quickly for Aretha. She recorded several albums before making her breakthrough in 1967 with two phenomenally successful records. That year, she also made her first European tour and appeared at New York City's Philharmonic Hall. Soon, everyone in the country was singing her songs, and her name became a household word. Aretha had become the "Queen of Soul."

During her distinguished career, Aretha has had 21 gold records and has won ten Grammy Awards. "Chain of Fools," "Never Loved a Man," "Respect," and "Natural Woman" are just a few of her popular songs. Shy and retiring off-stage, Aretha was nevertheless at the forefront of a new musical era in the 1960s when African-American or "Negro" music finally became acceptable and popular to both blacks and whites alike.

Today Aretha is still turning out hot songs and videos. She can also be heard singing the theme song of the successful television show, "A Different World."

Judith Jamison

Dancer and Choreographer
1944–
Birthplace: Philadelphia, Pennsylvania

There's no one else like you in the world.
Look what you can create!

Most female professional dancers are five feet, six inches in height or shorter. But Judith Jamison is five-feet, ten-inches tall—and when she dances, she creates a powerful yet graceful picture with her body. A lady with a strong, honest spirit, Judith enjoys inspiring people interested in dance.

At the age of six, young Judy began taking violin, piano, and ballet lessons. When she was 21, she joined the Alvin Ailey American Dance Theater, a dance company founded by an African-American choreographer, Alvin Ailey. As part of the Ailey troupe, Judith toured the world. Alvin Ailey was so impressed with her talent and spirit that he created a dance just for her. It was called *Cry*, and it made Judith even more famous.

In 1980, Judith retired from the Ailey Theater to pursue other projects. She starred in the Broadway musical, *Sophisticated Ladies*. She appeared as a guest dancer with, and choreographed dances for, many other dance companies. She also taught dance in schools and colleges. But Judith soon realized that she had even more to express creatively. So in 1988, she formed her own dance company called the Jamison Project. It was an immediate success.

Following Alvin Ailey's death in 1989, however, Judith was named artistic director of both the Alvin Ailey American Dance Theater and the Alvin Ailey American Dance Center—the official school of the Ailey company. She is one of the few women to hold such a prestigious position in a major dance company.

Judith Jamison, highly recognized for both her talent and her contributions to the art of dance, has won many prizes and awards. The Candace Award, presented to her in 1990 by the National Coalition of 100 Black Women, is only one of them. But to her, the greatest award is helping people all over the world experience and enjoy the art of dance.

Athletes

THE SPIRIT OF CHAMPIONS

Florence Griffith Joyner sprints to an Olympic world record in the 200-meter dash.

It took sheer determination to
be able to run a hundred yards
and remember all of the mechanics
that go along with it.
It takes steady nerves
and being a fighter to stay out there.

—Wilma Rudolph

Alice Coachman

Olympic Gold Medalist
1926–
Birthplace: Albany, Georgia

Alice Coachman won the high jump!

All children love to run and jump. Alice Coachman, however, found that she could run very fast and jump very high. When she was in the seventh grade, she vaulted five feet, four-and-one-half inches in the high jump, less than one inch from the world record mark! Once Alice accomplished this, the sports world began to watch her more closely to see what else she could do.

Alice soon established herself as one of the true great athletes in the history of amateur competition. When she was 13 years old, she entered the Amateur Athletic Union (AAU) competitions and won 22 individual titles. She won the outdoor AAU championships for nine years in a row, from 1939 to 1947—something no athlete had ever done before. In addition, Alice won the indoor championships in 1941, 1945, and 1946. As a sprinter, she won the 50-meter dash in every competition from 1942 through 1947. In 1944, she tied the world record for that event while setting a new American record of 6.4 seconds. In 1945 and 1946, she won the indoor 50-yard dash.

In 1948, Alice made the United States Women's Olympic Team, which competed at the World Olympics in London. This time when the fans screamed, "Alice Coachman won the high jump!" the phrase held an extra meaning. This time Alice's performance had made her the first African-American woman to win an Olympic gold medal for the high jump. Coaches, athletes, and fans of American track and field were all amazed by the accomplishments of the young 22-year-old African-American woman who had proven herself to be an outstanding sprinter and the best female high jumper in the country. With this victory, Alice Coachman became an inspiring hero to an entire generation of young African-American women and athletes.

Althea Gibson

She Kept Her Eye on the Ball
1927–
Birthplace: Silver, South Carolina

You got to know your opponent. You got to know their strengths, their weaknesses. . . .

When Althea Gibson was a child, many people believed that tennis was not a game that African Americans could play well. But Althea thought differently. She knew that anything was possible if she worked hard enough.

Althea was born in South Carolina, but she grew up in New York City. As a child, she played almost every sport imaginable: basketball, shuffleboard, volleyball, and paddle tennis. Paddle tennis is a game played with wooden paddles on street courts half the size of regular tennis courts. Althea liked to play paddle tennis with a friend and became so good at the sport, she won numerous medals in many competitions.

This brought her to the attention of Buddy Walker, a local coach. He bought Althea her first tennis racket and introduced her to the game of tennis. Since there were few tennis courts in her neighborhood, Althea practiced hitting balls on handball courts and on wood courts in Harlem. She was determined to learn the game and become successful.

In 1950, at age 23, Althea became the first African American to play the U.S. Open tennis competition. The following year she became the first African American to play Wimbledon in England. Six years later she became the first black tennis player ever to win the Wimbledon championship, after which she returned home to Harlem to a ticker-tape parade put on in her honor. Later, in 1957, Althea won the women's singles title at the U.S. Open. In 1958, she repeated her Wimbledon and U.S. Open wins.

By working hard and overcoming the odds, Althea Gibson became the first black person to win major titles in tennis. She also became an international tennis star and an inspiration to all women. Today there is still not a significant number of blacks playing professional tennis. But Arthur Ashe, Zina Garrison, and all the other black tennis players owe a debt of gratitude to Althea. Her pioneering efforts made their way a little easier.

Wilma Rudolph

Beauty in Motion
1940–
Birthplace: Clarksville, Tennessee

I would be very disappointed if I were only remembered as a runner because I feel that my contribution to the youth of America has far exceeded the woman who was the Olympic champion. The challenge is still there.

T he effects of scarlet fever and polio left Wilma Rudolph crippled at the age of four. She had to wear a brace on her left leg. But Wilma was determined to walk and run again without the brace. Her large family, which included 22 children, helped her and encouraged her efforts. By the time she was eight, Wilma no longer needed the brace. By age 11, Wilma was finally able to run and play like all the other kids.

Wilma never liked to lose. She always tried very hard to be a winner—and her determined spirit usually led her to success. Always involved in sports, she won many races in high school and she was also a star basketball player. In 1956, she scored 803 points during one season. Because of her outstanding athletic ability, Tennessee State University gave Wilma a scholarship to run on their track team.

In July 1960, the year of the Olympics, Wilma set the world record for 200 meters. Several months later, at the Olympics in Rome, Italy, she became the first woman to ever win three gold medals in track. Her accomplishments earned her the reputation of being the fastest woman runner in the world. That year, the news media honored Wilma by making her "Athlete of the Year."

But when Wilma returned home from the Olympics, she turned her energy to more sensitive issues. When her town tried to put on a parade in Wilma's honor, she told them that she would not attend a parade that would be segregated. Her town complied with her request, and the parade was open to all. Wilma had broken through another barrier.

Wilma Rudolph's concern for her people did not stop there. She is credited with promoting interest in sports among young women. Olympic coach Nell Jackson said, "Wilma's accomplishments opened up the real door for women in track because of her grace and beauty." Wilma formed the Wilma Rudolph Foundation to help underprivileged children. She is now a special consultant on minority affairs at De Pauw University in Indiana.

Florence Griffith Joyner

Star of Track and Field
1959–
Birthplace: Los Angeles, California

Sprinting is excitement.

Florence's interest in running began before she was seven years old. To amuse herself during visits to her father, who lived in the Mojave Desert, Florence would chase jackrabbits. Jackrabbits are among the fastest animals on earth. In 1963, at age seven, the sprint training she did with the rabbits allowed her to win a Sugar Ray Robinson Youth Foundation Competition held in Los Angeles. And that was the beginning of her athletic career.

Florence attended Jordan High School in Los Angeles where she set school records in the sprints and the long jump. After graduation in 1978, she enrolled at California State University and began studying for her business degree. There she excelled in academic subjects as well as athletics, and it was there that she met Bobby Kersee, Cal State's exceptional track coach. Kersee helped develop her skill as a runner. She was so loyal to Bobby Kersee that when he left Cal State for the University of California, Los Angeles (UCLA), Florence followed.

Because of her impressive athletic performance at UCLA, Florence was invited to the United States Olympic Trials in 1980. She did not make the team. Florence's defeat only made her try harder, and in 1984 she made it.

From the time she was five years old, Florence liked to dress creatively. When she became a member of the Olympic team, she was no different. She competed in shimmering bodysuits and long fingernails, which earned her the nickname "Fluorescent Flo." During the 1984 Olympics, she won a silver medal for her second-place finish in the 200-meter dash.

Between 1987 and 1988, Florence's power as a sprinter developed into an awesome force. By that time she had met and married Al Joyner, a 1984 Olympic medalist, who became her workout partner and supervisor. Together they worked for the 1988 Olympics in Seoul, South Korea, where Florence once again proved her skill by winning three gold medals. Now known as FloJo, the little girl who chased jackrabbits has caught the attention of the world.

Cheryl Miller

Basketball Champion
1964-
Birthplace: Riverside, California

*My definition of losing is not somebody who
loses a game. . . . Losing is giving
up. . . . Everyone can be a winner in life.*

E veryone in Cheryl Miller's hometown knew that she excelled in the sport of basketball. At Riverside Polytechnic High School, Cheryl's talent earned her such awards as Player of the Year, Most Valuable Player, High School Player of the Year, and AAU All-American. Cheryl was fun to watch, too, because she loved to entertain the audience with good-natured antics on the court.

After graduating from high school, Cheryl attended the University of Southern California (USC). She studied telecommunications in preparation for a career in television. Cheryl also continued to play basketball on the USC women's team and broke records in scoring, rebounding, field goals, free throws, and steals. With her help, USC won national championships in 1983 and 1984.

Cheryl won many awards during her college basketball years also, like the 1984–1985 ESPN Woman Athlete of the Year Award. She also helped the American women win a gold medal at the Goodwill Games in 1986.

Cheryl attracted much attention off the court, too. She gave a lot of her time to acting as a spokesperson for organizations that help children and young adults: the Muscular Dystrophy Association, the Los Angeles Literacy Campaign, and Athletes for Kids. She was the commissioner of the 1985 Los Angeles Olympic Committee Summer Youth Games. A role model for many teenage girls, Cheryl often speaks to groups of high school students, encouraging them to get an education, stay away from drugs, and follow their dreams. Cheryl was so well liked that Mayor Tom Bradley proclaimed December 12, 1986, Cheryl Miller Day in the city of Los Angeles.

After she graduated from college, Cheryl Miller was signed as commentator for the ABC television network, where she can now be seen reporting on college basketball games and other events.

Entrepreneurs

TAKING CARE OF BUSINESS

Television producer Oprah Winfrey on the set of her famous talk show.

I am the product of every other black woman
before me who has done or said anything worthwhile.
Recognizing that I am a part of history
is what allows me to soar.

—Oprah Winfrey

Biddy Mason

From Slave to Wealthy Landowner
1818–1891
Birthplace: Mississippi or Georgia
(exact birthplace unknown)

If you hold your hand closed, nothing good can come in. The open hand is blessed, for it gives abundance, even as it receives.

Bridget Mason was a slave who belonged to the Smith family in Mississippi. As a slave, she was forbidden to read or write, but she was able to learn traditional African, Caribbean, and Western medicine from older midwives and slave doctors. This knowledge would later prove invaluable to "Biddy."

In 1851, Smith moved his family and slaves to California. Traveling by wagon and riverboat, the trip took almost a year. Biddy was not allowed to ride in the wagon with the others. Her job was to walk behind the rest of the caravan and keep the farm animals from straying. So Biddy actually made the trip from Mississippi to California on foot.

In moving across the country, Smith had made a grave mistake: California prohibited slavery. As soon as he discovered this, Smith tried to move his 14 slaves out of state. Some alert African Americans stopped Smith and took him to court. Although Biddy was not permitted to testify, she bravely cooperated by telling her story to the judge privately. Smith's slaves won their case and their freedom in 1856.

Once free, Biddy settled in Los Angeles, where she was offered a job as a midwife and nurse. She soon became a familiar figure, carrying her large black medical bag through the dusty, unpaved streets. Her expert skills as a midwife made her famous. She delivered hundreds of babies for families rich and poor, black and white.

After ten years, Biddy had saved enough money to buy land just outside of town. There she established a family homestead. The purchase proved to be a wise investment. As the city of Los Angeles grew, her land became more valuable. In time, she bought more property. Biddy became so wealthy that she was able to help the poor and newly arrived settlers of all races. There was always a line of needy people outside her door, even on the day she died.

Biddy Mason was one of the first black women in Los Angeles to own property. Her original homestead has been preserved and is now a historical site.

Madame C.J. Walker

**First Black Female Millionaire
1867–1919
Birthplace: Delta, Louisiana**

I am a woman who came from the cotton fields of the South. I was promoted from there to the washtub. Then I was promoted to the cook kitchen, and from there I promoted myself into the business of manufacturing hair goods and preparations. . . . I have built my own factory on my own ground.

Madame C.J. Walker was born Sarah Breedlove, the daughter of former slaves. She married at the age of 14 and became Sarah McWilliams. When her husband died, Sarah moved to St. Louis, Missouri. There she became a washerwoman and attended school at night. During this time, Sarah's hair began to fall out, and nothing she tried would stop it.

One night Sarah had a dream. She dreamed about a cure for her hair loss. Later she found the ingredients, mixed them together, and tried the mixture on her hair. The formula was a success. Sarah started selling her new product door to door and eventually expanded her business to Denver, Colorado. There, in 1905, she married a newspaper man named Charles Walker. She began calling herself Madame C.J. Walker, and has been known by that name ever since.

Madame Walker became famous for her hair-care products. She is best known for inventing the pressing comb and a conditioner for straightening hair. At that time, black women thought having straight hair was more beautiful than hair left in its natural state. Today many hair styles have become acceptable, in part because of Madame Walker's role in setting a standard for black beauty that has helped to raise the self-esteem of black women.

In 1910, Madame Walker established a factory in Indianapolis where she employed 5,000 black women. An active community leader, Madame Walker also gave thousands of dollars to the Tuskegee Institute, the NAACP, and other black charities. She also helped establish the Mary McLeod Bethune School, now known as Bethune-Cookman College in Daytona, Florida.

Using her determination and energy, Madame Walker followed her dream and became America's first black female millionaire. When she died in her New York mansion, she left an estate valued at two million dollars.

Maggie Lena Walker

First American Woman Bank President
1867–1934
Birthplace: Richmond, Virginia

I am of the opinion [that] if we can catch the vision, in a few years we shall be able to enjoy the fruits from this effort and its attendant responsibilities, through untold benefits reaped by the youth of the race.

After Reconstruction, Maggie Lena Mitchell lived in dire poverty. Her situation was like that of most African Americans at that time. But despite being poor, Maggie's mother, a house slave for a wealthy woman, made sure her daughter attended school in Richmond, Virginia.

After graduating from high school at 16, Maggie began teaching. Soon after, she accepted a job as secretary of the Independent Order of St. Luke Society in Richmond. The Order of St. Luke assisted sick and elderly members and paid for burial and funeral services.

In 1899, Maggie was named secretary-treasurer. Under her direction, the order increased its membership tremendously by encouraging many other black women to manage and save their money. On behalf of the order, Maggie acquired a $100,000 office building, increased the staff to 55, and established a bank that became the Consolidated Bank and Trust Company. She served as chairman of the board and became the first woman in the United States to direct a bank.

Always willing to extend a helping hand to the poor black people of Richmond, Maggie was the first to start a number of other businesses. She founded an insurance company, a black newspaper, the *St. Luke Herald*, and a school and home for delinquent girls. She promoted the establishment of a community center that provided better health care for African Americans and continued to serve on the boards of many civic groups.

Maggie was a great admirer of Booker T. Washington, and she took his advice to heart. "Cast down your bucket where you are," he said to all African Americans, and Maggie did. In doing so, her achievements not only served to benefit the African-American people of Virginia, but enhanced the entire city of Richmond. In her honor, the city government named a street, a theater, and a high school after this remarkable woman.

Susan Taylor

The *Essence* Woman
1946–
Birthplace: New York, New York

Our parents and the preceding generations of African people . . . didn't allow their fears and doubts to immobilize them. They took action. . . . All we need, all that our people need, begins with you and me. Get organized. Get busy. . . . We must move forward: . . . We haven't come this far not to go the distance.

Actress; wife; mother; cosmetologist; editor-in-chief, *Essence* magazine; vice president, Essence Communications, Inc. Those are the roles that Susan Taylor has played— and continues to play—with intelligence, vitality, and sensitivity.

In the 1960s Susan was an actress with the Negro Ensemble Company, pursuing a demanding career. Her daughter's birth in 1969 made Susan realize that she would have to divert time away from acting to care for her child. So Susan went into business. She became a licensed beautician and created her own line of cosmetics: Nequai Cosmetics.

The success of Nequai Cosmetics and Susan's expertise in cosmetology came to the attention of the editors of *Essence*. In 1970, she began working for *Essence* as a freelance writer. By 1971 Susan became the magazine's beauty editor, and by 1972 she supervised both the fashion and beauty departments. Hard work and discipline characterized both Susan's acting and business careers. Those qualities also typified her performance as *Essence* magazine's beauty and fashion editor.

Since 1981 Susan has been the magazine's editor-in-chief. One of her responsibilities in that position is writing the monthly editorial, "In the Spirit." Through her editorials she promotes positive images of black women and shares her thoughts on those values she holds important. Susan has used her strengths to set a positive course for her life. She is committed to helping the poor, women in prison, and teenage mothers do the same.

In recognition of her outstanding performance as editor-in-chief of *Essence*, Susan has received many awards including the Women in Communications Matrix Award and an honorary Doctorate of Humane Letters from Lincoln University (1988). In 1986, Susan became a vice president of Essence Communications, Inc.

Suzanne de Passe

First Lady of Motown
1946–
Birthplace: New York, New York

I definitely was aware that I was black, but I also was aware that I had ability and hope and promise.

I n 1968, 23-year-old Suzanne de Passe convinced her new boss, Berry Gordy of Motown Records, to sign and develop a new act. It was the Jackson Five, starring the then nine-year-old Michael Jackson. Then she convinced the label to sign the Commodores with their lead singer, Lionel Ritchie.

Such advice made Suzanne de Passe, a former concert promoter, an indispensable part of Motown Records. Her ability to spot talent and to promote Motown's musical groups made her a powerhouse in the music industry. Her influence, however, did not stop there. After 13 years with the record division, Gordy moved Suzanne into the company's motion picture division. She was put in charge of all television, movie, cable, video, and stage production. Living up to the challenge, Suzanne won an NAACP Image Award and two Emmy Awards for two of the major television specials she produced for Motown. They were "Motown 25," which celebrated the 25th anniversary of the famous record label, and "Motown Returns to the Apollo," a salute to the Apollo Theater.

Even as a little girl, Suzanne knew that her life would be glamorous. "I absolutely pictured myself climbing in and out of limousines," she has said. Growing up in Harlem, in a middle-class family, Suzanne had the luxury of attending private schools. This, she says, helped give her the self-confidence and assurance she needed to succeed.

Suzanne de Passe, now president of Gordy/dePasse Productions (previously Motown Productions), has been credited with keeping her company alive by moving Motown firmly into television. She is in charge of a $65-million budget to produce feature films and television programs. Among her most recent productions are the TV movies "The Jacksons: An American Dream" and the Emmy Award-winning "Lonesome Dove."

Phyllis Tucker Vinson

Caretaker of Children's Television
1948–
Birthplace: Los Angeles, California

I think power can be abused and I try not to abuse it; I try to be diplomatic and fair. I don't forget who I am. If I give [my job] up, who is going to do it, as far as minorities and women are concerned?

In 1969, Phyllis Tucker Vinson was an unwed mother of a baby boy who had to support her child with welfare assistance. In 1989, she was NBC's vice president of children's and family programming, making a substantial salary and a substantial contribution to America.

Underneath Phyllis's rags-to-riches story is a major factor: she was a determined woman. Her middle-class family did not approve of her decision to go on welfare, but, Phyllis says, "It was my mistake, and I said to them, 'Let me take care of it.' "

Struggling to make ends meet, Phyllis worked hard to get her bachelor's degree in child development at California State University in Los Angeles. After graduation, she took a job as a secretary at NBC. She intended to leave the television company when she received her teaching credentials. But Phyllis didn't leave. Instead, she discovered that she loved her work and quickly rose through the network's corporate ranks. In 1979, she became a director of children's programming.

Phyllis has accomplished much during her career. She brought the successful "Smurfs," "Alvin and the Chipmunks," and the animated "Punky Brewster" to the TV screen. This helped NBC receive the number-one rating in its children's lineup for six years.

Now the mother of five children, Phyllis is more concerned than ever about the state of children's television. While at NBC, her goal was to improve television programming for children by focusing on the concerns of African Americans and other minorities on screen and off. For this she has received many honors, including the NAACP Medgar Evers Community Service Award. In her new position as executive vice president of World Africa Network, Phyllis hopes to produce family shows that will even more truthfully depict the experiences of the world's African people.

Oprah Winfrey

Talk Show Queen
1954–
Birthplace: Kosciusko, Mississippi

*[E]xcellence is the best deterrent
to racism or sexism.*

As a child Oprah Winfrey was known as "the little speaker." At age two, she addressed a church congregation on the topic of "Jesus rose on Easter Day." At age 12, she delivered another speech in church and was paid $500. That was when Oprah knew what she wanted to do for a living: she wanted to be "paid to talk."

In spite of her natural communication abilities, Oprah's childhood was difficult. When her parents separated, Oprah was sent to live with her strict maternal grandmother on a farm. At age six, she joined her mother and her two half-brothers in a Milwaukee ghetto. Without a parent constantly around to watch out for her, Oprah was sexually abused by male relatives from the age of nine to 13. As Oprah grew more angry, she became more rebellious, so her mother sent her to live with her father in Nashville, Tennessee.

"My father saved my life," Oprah has said. A barber and city councilman, Vernon Winfrey was a disciplinarian who insisted that Oprah do well in school. As a result, when she was 16, she won a full scholarship to Tennessee State University. While still in college, Oprah was offered a job with CBS, and at the age of 19 became Nashville's first black female co-anchor on the evening news.

A series of news reporting jobs followed, and then, in 1984, Oprah became the host of "AM Chicago." By 1985, the show was expanded to an hour and renamed "The Oprah Winfrey Show." When the show was aired nationally, it won three Emmy Awards, and Oprah became famous. Since then, the show has won five more Emmys and four NAACP Image Awards. In addition, Oprah has won an Academy Award nomination for her acting debut in the movie *The Color Purple*.

Oprah became so successful that she formed a production company, Harpo Productions, and bought her show. Forming this company makes Oprah the first woman in history to own and produce her own talk show. Her company has produced many television movies and series, including "The Women of Brewster Place," which tried to portray truthful images of African American life. Oprah is now one of the most influential African Americans and women in television.

Lawyers & Policy Makers

FORGING EQUAL JUSTICE

Elizabeth Eckford, one of the Little Rock Nine, calmly walks past
shouting mobs into Central High School in 1957.

*You could say that race was an obstacle to me,
you could say that sex was an obstacle to me,
but I refused to own them in that way.
I was black and female, but I never conceived
that those were supposed to
keep me from doing what I wanted to do.*

—Eleanor Holmes Norton

Charlotte E. Ray

First Black Woman Lawyer
1850–1911
Birthplace: New York, New York

. . . a colored woman who read us a thesis on corporations, not copied from the books but from her brain, a clear incisive analysis of one of the most delicate legal questions.

—Howard University President's Report, 1870

Charlotte was one of seven children born to Charlotte Augusta Burroughs Ray and the Reverend Charles Bennett Ray. Reverend Ray was a well-known abolitionist and an important contact in the Underground Railroad. As a child, Charlotte attended the Institution for the Education of Colored Youth in Washington D.C. There she excelled at her studies and by 1869, at age 19, she was a teacher in the Normal and Preparatory Department at Howard University.

While at Howard, Charlotte made good use of her time. She taught by day and studied law there at night. How honored, proud, and joyful Charlotte must have felt when, in February 1872, she received her law degree from Howard, the first black woman in the United States to attain that goal! Two months later, Charlotte must have experienced those feelings again when she became the first woman to be admitted to the bar in Washington, D.C. Now Charlotte could practice law, and within a month of being licensed she was doing just that.

Self-confident and determined, Charlotte took another step forward and opened her own law practice. This time, however, public prejudice worked against her. Although she was an excellent lawyer, she was black and female, and could not attract enough clients to keep her law practice going. She closed her office.

Charlotte continued to serve her people through activities in other organizations. In 1876, she attended the Annual Convention of the National Women's Suffrage Association in New York and, after 1895, became active in the National Association of Colored Women. In 1879, Charlotte returned to New York City where she taught in the Brooklyn Public Schools.

In 1897, she moved to Woodside, Long Island. There she died at age 60 from acute bronchitis. Although racial and gender prejudice stopped Charlotte from achieving the success as a lawyer that she deserved, her accomplishments served to encourage many other black women to study law.

Edith Sampson

United Nations Delegate
1901–1980
Birthplace: Pittsburgh, Pennsylvania

The airplane, the radio, films, and the free press . . . are modern instruments for building a people's front against aggression. . . . Let's use them with all the energy and imagination we can muster.

For Edith Sampson, obtaining an education was not easy. Because of family financial problems, Edith was forced to drop out of grade school and go to work. But she understood all too well the need for education, so Edith went back to school later and received her high school diploma.

After she graduated, an organization called the Associated Charities hired Edith and arranged for her to attend the New York School of Social Work. There she excelled at a required course in criminology. Because of her outstanding performance, her law professor urged Edith to become a lawyer.

Continuing to work as a social worker in Chicago, Edith took that professor's advice and started studying law at night at the John Marshall Law School. She received her bachelor of laws degree in 1925 and then in 1927 earned her master of laws degree from Loyola University in Illinois. Edith became the first woman to receive such a degree from that institution.

Upon graduation, Edith established her own law practice in Chicago's South Side and became a probation officer and referee on the juvenile court of Cook County. She held those positions for 18 year while she continued to practice law, specializing in criminal law and domestic relations.

In 1949, as chairperson of the National Council of Negro Women's executive committee, Edith was one of 26 American leaders who took part in the World Town Hall of the Air lecture tour. The group visited over 20 countries and participated in public debates on current political issues. After this extensive tour, President Harry Truman recognized Edith's qualifications and appointed her to serve as alternate delegate to the United Nations General Assembly in 1950. Edith became the first African American to hold that position. She was frequently sent abroad as a guest lecturer. Her speeches often stressed the need for equal rights for all people, an issue that is still important today.

Shirley Chisholm

First Black Congresswoman
1924–
Birthplace: Brooklyn, New York

Your time is now, my sisters. . . .New goals and new priorities, not only for this country, but for all mankind, must be set.

S hirley St. Hill's parents left Barbados hoping to make a better life for themselves in the United States. But in the 1920s, making a good living was difficult for black people, so Shirley's parents sent their three daughters back to Barbados to live with their grandmother. Shirley, the eldest, was three years old.

When she was nine, Shirley and her sisters returned to the United States to live with their parents. An outspoken child, Shirley excelled in her Brooklyn school just as she had in Barbados.

Shirley's first exposure to politics came when she was a student at Brooklyn College. There she heard many white politicians speak. An unflattering comment about black leadership from one such politician fired Shirley's desire to prove to white America that African Americans are as capable of leadership as anyone.

After graduating with a degree in education, Shirley taught at a nursery school while she took courses at Columbia University toward her master's degree. During that time, she met and married Conrad Chisholm, a Jamaican private investigator.

Ever concerned about the people of Brooklyn, Shirley set up day-care centers for the working mothers. The centers were so successful that Brooklyn residents chose Shirley to represent them in the New York State legislature in 1964. Then, in 1968, Shirley was chosen to represent them in the United States Congress. She became the first African-American congresswoman and served for seven terms, from 1968 to 1982.

Shirley was not afraid to voice her opinions in Washington, D.C. She wanted the poor people of the United States to live good lives. She wanted equality for all. The only person with enough power to achieve these goals is the President of the United States. So in 1972, Shirley decided to run for President and campaigned to win the Democratic party nomination. Shirley lost the bid, but she established another first for black America and a first for the women of America.

Constance Baker Motley

Lawyer of Distinction
1921–
Birthplace: New Haven, Connecticut

When you see black people on television brushing their teeth with Colgate like everybody else, that says much more than any civil rights activist or orator.

C onstance was born in the small state of Connecticut, but the legal battles she won made a big difference in the lives of her people. Constance began her legal career working for the NAACP Legal Defense and Educational Fund in 1945. She eventually became one of its associate counsels. During her association with this important organization, she won nine out of the ten cases that she argued before the United States Supreme Court. She also participated in almost every case brought before the courts during that time.

One of Constance's most famous victories won James Meredith the right to become a student at the University of Mississippi. Prior to that court decision, it was against the law for African-American and white students in Mississippi to attend college together. Many states, especially in the South, had enacted laws that discriminated against African Americans. A 1896 United States Supreme court decision supported these statutes. Battles like the James Meredith case had to be won to strike down these unfair laws.

After Constance left the NAACP Legal Defense and Educational Fund in 1965, she decided to pursue a career in politics. In doing so, she continued to break down barriers. She was elected to the New York State Senate, the first African-American woman in the state's history to do so. In 1965, she became the first African American and first woman to be elected to the powerful office of Manhattan borough president in New York City. In 1966, President Lyndon Johnson made her the first African-American woman federal judge when he appointed her to the United States District Court for Southern New York State. In June 1982, Constance was named chief judge of the Federal District Court that covers Manhattan, the Bronx, and six counties north of New York City.

Using the courts and the law as her weapons, Constance Baker Motley remains vigilant in the fight for justice.

Cardiss Collins

A Natural Politician
1931–
Birthplace: St. Louis, Missouri

Fighting bigotry, racism, and discrimination has been a prevalent factor throughout my adult life. . . .we should overcome the tradition of racism . . . and rise above the expectation of the founding fathers . . . to truly experience a democracy.

When she was ten, Cardiss and her family moved from St. Louis, Missouri, to Detroit, Michigan. Upon graduation from Detroit High School of Commerce, Cardiss went to Chicago to attend Northwestern University.

It was in Chicago that Cardiss's interest in politics came to light. There she met and married George Collins, a rising politician. While George served as a Chicago alderman and committeeman, Cardiss served on the committee of Chicago's 24th Ward Regular Democratic Organization and became deeply involved with her husband's career at the same time.

In 1970, George was elected as a Democrat to the U.S. House of Representatives, representing the Seventh District in Illinois. Cardiss was so involved with her husband's work that when he died in a plane crash in 1972, she became the best candidate to fill his unexpired term of office.

Cardiss proved to be a natural and concerned politician. She is dedicated to representing the interests of her district, which is 68 percent African American. Her popularity among her constituents was most evident in 1988 when she ran unopposed in the congressional election.

In Congress, Cardiss serves on several committees and has achieved many firsts: She is the first woman and the first black person to chair the House Government Operations Subcommittee on Manpower and Housing. In addition, Cardiss was the first woman to chair the Congressional Black Caucus (1978–1980), and was the first black and first woman to hold a Democratic leadership position in the House of Representatives when she was named whip-at-large.

With an unfailing sense of devotion, Cardiss has focused on issues that will improve the welfare of her people. She has served in Congress for more than 17 years—making her the longest-serving black woman in Congress. Her strong and effective leadership may well keep her in office for many years to come.

Yvonne Braithwaite Burke

California's First Black Congresswoman
1932–
Birthplace: Los Angeles, California

When I walk into a room I assume I have to prove myself. I know that. . . .But I also know that I can prove myself.

Yvonne Braithwaite Burke is used to being a "first." She was the first and only child of her janitor father and real-estate agent mother. She was the first black student to attend a model school at the University of Southern California. She was one of the first two African-American girls in a women's honor society at her high school. She was the first black woman elected to the California General Assembly and the first to be elected to the United States Congress. Once there she became the first representative ever to be granted maternity leave.

Born Pearl Yvonne Watson (she dropped the name Pearl because she didn't like it), this high achiever has her roots in the East side of Los Angeles. Although she grew up poor, she did not grow up underpriviledged. Her hard-working parents supported and encouraged her in all her endeavors, supplying her with as many extracurricular activities as they could afford.

But even loving and attentive parents could not shield Yvonne from the injustices of racism and sexism. After receiving her bachelor's degree from the University of California at Los Angeles and her law degree from the University of Southern California, Yvonne found it impossible to find a position in a law firm. At that time no blacks, women, or Jews were being hired by white law firms.

Rather than becoming dejected, Yvonne looked around for opportunities that were open to her. She found them in government. Prior to her election to Congress, Yvonne served as a California State Assemblywoman for six years. She then served three two-year terms in the U.S. Congress.

Yvonne strove to fight such discrimination through the legislative process and achieved enormous success. Yvonne has said, "I wanted everything," and never doubting her abilities, she got everything she ever wanted. This lawyer and politician is also a wife, mother, and, finally, a partner in a successful corporate law firm.

Barbara Jordan

First Black Southern Congressperson
1936—
Birthplace: Houston, Texas

My approach is to respect the humanity of everybody.

Barbara Charline Jordan listened in awe as Edith Sampson, a black woman lawyer from Chicago, spoke. It was career day at Barbara's high school, and before this day began Barbara didn't know what she wanted to do with her life. Now, after listening to this dynamic woman, Barbara knew: She would become an attorney.

Soon thereafter Barbara was traveling in segregated buses—sitting on the seats labeled "colored"—to attend college at Texas Southern University. After graduating with her bachelor's degree, she went North to study at Boston University for her law degree. Barbara was earnest in her belief that she could make her mark in law.

"I always wanted to be something unusual," Barbara has said. "I never wanted to be run-of-the-mill." Indeed Barbara Jordan's life and career have not been ordinary. Her accomplishments as a lawmaker are outstanding. She began practicing law in her hometown of Houston and became a county judge's assistant. A few years later she was elected to the Texas State Senate, the first African American to sit there since 1883. After serving on most of the major Senate committees, Barbara ran for Congress and became the first black congressperson to be elected from the Deep South since the turn of the century. She served three very successful terms of office.

Because of her accomplishments, many civil rights leaders wanted Barbara to join them in their organizations to fight for justice for African Americans. But seeing herself as a lawmaker first and foremost, Barbara preferred to make changes within the legal and governmental systems. "I am telling the young people that if you're dissatisfied with the way things are, then you have to resolve to change them. I am telling them to get out there and occupy these positions in government and make the decisions; do the job and make it work for you."

Barbara has been a professor at the University of Texas since 1979. She is currently the special advisor on ethics to the governor of Texas.

Eleanor Holmes Norton

Civil Rights Lawyer
1937–
Birthplace: Washington, D.C.

One ought to struggle for its own sake. One ought to be against racism and sexism because they are wrong, not because one is black or one is female.

Eleanor Holmes Norton was born and raised in Washington, D.C., where four generations of her family have lived. As a child, Eleanor was an achiever with a strong sense of responsibility. She was encouraged, perhaps, by the fact that she was the oldest of three girls. Although she admits that she did not know what career to pursue when she was an undergraduate at Antioch College, becoming a civil rights lawyer felt like the right course for her to take. So Eleanor went on with her studies at Yale University and received a master's degree in American history and a law degree at the same time. She accomplished this "for no other reason except that you want to stretch your mind," she has said.

From the moment Eleanor became an attorney, she worked steadfastly to oppose discrimination of any kind. She spent five years working with the American Civil Liberities Union helping to protect the basic constitutional rights of all Americans. She was then appointed chairperson of the New York City Commission on Human Rights. She held this position for seven years.

Then, in 1977, President Jimmy Carter appointed Eleanor chairperson of the Equal Employment Opportunity Commission. This federal agency was created to end discrimination based on sex, race, religion, or national origin in the hiring practices of businesses.

Eleanor was the first woman to chair that committee and she held that position until 1981. Since 1982, she has been a professor at the Georgetown University Law Center in Washington, D.C. In November 1990, Eleanor became the second person and the first woman elected to represent the District of Columbia in the United States House of Representatives.

Although being black and female were obstacles she had to face, they never stopped Eleanor from achieving her goals. Instead, she used her own experience as a black woman to speak passionately for her clients, for civil rights, and for the betterment of her country.

Maxine Waters

California Powerbroker
1939–
Birthplace: St. Louis, Missouri

Some people say I'm feisty. Some say I'm tough. Combative. Bitchy. In the community where I come from—the community of survival—those were considered good qualities.

Maxine was born in St. Louis, Missouri, the fifth of 13 children. Raised in a single-parent home, life for young Maxine was full of hand-me-downs, of welfare assistance, and an ongoing struggle to make ends meet.

In addition to these hardships, Maxine was constantly compared to her three older sisters, whom everyone thought were prettier. But instead of making Maxine feel inferior, the hurtful comparisons only served to make her try harder and achieve more. Fortunately, she received a lot of support in school. She was often chosen to represent her class and her school in various events, so it was natural and fitting for a classmate to predict in Maxine's senior yearbook that she would one day be Speaker of the U.S. House of Representatives.

After high school, however, Maxine immediately got married and had two children. Five years later, she found herself in Los Angeles, broke. Her husband found work in a factory, and Maxine labored in the garment district. Then, in 1966, a friend told her about a federal program called Head Start. Maxine started there as a teaching assistant, but quickly discovered that she worked better with the parents than the children.

That was the beginning of Maxine's activism and the start of her political career. She found that she enjoyed helping people and that she had a natural talent for politics. She went back to college, divorced her husband, and worked as a political volunteer, which led to other paid political positions.

In 1976, Maxine ran for the state assembly and won. For 14 years she represented the 48th district in South Central Los Angeles and was considered one of the most effective African Americans in the California political arena. In November 1990, Maxine was elected to the United States House of Representatives from the State of California. She now has the opportunity to make that yearbook inscription come true.

Scientists & Healers

EXPLORING WITHOUT BOUNDARIES

Mae C. Jemison wears a 300 lb. space suit in preparation for "space walk" training.

*Failure to recognize possiblities is the
most dangerous and common mistake
one can make. Don't limit yourself
because of others' limited imagination.
Never limit another because of your
limited imagination.*

—Mae C. Jemison

Mary Eliza Mahoney

First Black Graduate Nurse
1845–1926
Birthplace: Boston, Massachusetts

During [Mary Mahoney's] 40 years in nursing she provided exemplary care and made outstanding contributions to nursing organizations.

—The American Nurses' Association

Before the latter part of the 19th century, many American nurses were untrained. Since doctors were often not available, these women delivered babies and provided folk remedies for illnesses. In the North and South, many of these nurses were black. African-American women have long been nurses and midwives in the United States. Yet when nursing schools started opening after the Civil War, black women were usually not allowed to attend them.

Mary Eliza Mahoney was an exception. She was the first African-American woman to graduate from a professional white nursing school. Mary's interest in nursing began when, as the oldest daughter in a family of 25, she acted as the midwife at the births of her younger brothers and sisters. But it wasn't until she was 33 years old that she was accepted at the New England Hospital for Women and Children in Boston, the first American school to introduce a nursing program. Dr. Marie Zakrzewska was the head of the school, and she was a firm believer in equal rights for women and for blacks. Under her guidance, six black nurses graduated by 1899. Mary Mahoney was the first.

The nursing course lasted 16 months, and Mary, a small, energetic young woman, worked 16 hours a day, seven days a week. She washed, ironed, cleaned, scrubbed, and studied, which was what all the student nurses were expected to do. The courses and the physical work were so difficult, only three women graduated out of that class of 40—two white women and Mary.

Mary worked as a nurse for 40 years after her graduation in 1879, constantly trying to help other graduate nurses at the same time. For her ceaseless efforts in the field of nursing and in the organization of nurses, the National Association of Colored Graduate Nurses established the Mary Mahoney Award in 1936. This award is now given to those African-American nurses who have contributed much to their profession—like Mary Mahoney did over one hundred years ago.

Rebecca J. Cole

Pioneer Physician
1846–1922
Birthplace: Unknown

We must attack the system of overcrowding in the poor districts by urging our men to contend for laws regulating the number [of people] in one dwelling . . . that people may not be crowded together like cattle while soulless landlords collect fifty percent in their investments.

In the mid-18th century, women—black and white—who were forced to live under the domination of males, started to assert themselves. Many wanted to receive training in professions that were formerly only practiced by men. Medicine was one such profession, and, in 1849, Elizabeth Blackwell became the first white woman doctor to receive her medical degree. Fifteen years later, Rebecca Lee—an African-American woman—graduated from New England Medical College. She was closely followed by Rebecca Cole—also an African-American woman—who graduated from Woman's Medical College of Pennsylvania in 1867.

There is much speculation as to which doctor, Rebecca Lee or Rebecca Cole, was the first black woman physician to practice in the United States. Both were equally accomplished, but Rebecca Cole achieved some prominence for her work with Elizabeth Blackwell.

After graduating, Rebecca Cole joined Elizabeth at the New York Infirmary for Women and Children. In addition to running the infirmary, Elizabeth and her sister Emily had started the Blackwell's Tenement House Service in 1866, which was the first medical social-service program to be started in the United States. Rebecca Cole was one of the service's first "sanitary visitors." She made house calls to people living in slum neighborhoods and taught women the basics of good hygiene and child care.

As a result of her experience with the Blackwells, when Rebecca returned to Philadelphia, she continued her career in social medicine. She helped start the Woman's Directory, which provided medical and legal assistance to women. She practiced medicine in Philadelphia until 1881. Later she became the superintendent of the Home for Destitute Colored Women and Children in Washington, D.C.

Rebecca was outspoken about the state of black health care. When W.E.B. Du Bois publicly stated that he felt blacks died of consumption in such high numbers because of their ignorance of hygiene, Rebecca disagreed, blaming slum landlords instead for the high mortality rates in the poor areas. Rebecca Cole practiced medicine for 50 years.

Susie King Taylor

Civil War Nurse
1848–1912
Birthplace: Isle of Wight, Georgia

[O]thers of our boys, some with their legs off, arm gone, foot off, and wounds of all kinds. They had to wade through creeks and marshes as they were discovered by the enemy and shelled very badly. A number of the men were lost....The 103rd New York suffered the most, as their men were very bady wounded. My work now began.

Susie Baker was raised by her grandmother in Savannah, Georgia. Even though she was born into slavery and was not allowed an education, she was taught how to read and write by a free black woman. Understanding how important education was, Susie used her skills to teach other African Americans at the Freedman's School when she was 14 years old. At that time, the Civil War had just started.

In 1862, Abraham Lincoln signed the Emancipation Proclamation that legally abolished slavery and set all African Americans free. Even though black soldiers were not allowed to fight alongside white soldiers and were treated badly, they fought bravely for their freedom and for their country.

Susie's husband, Edward King, was one of those soldiers. After they married in 1862, they moved to Port Royal Island off the South Carolina coast where Edward joined the First South Carolina volunteers, an all-black army regiment. This regiment was made up of former slaves from the Sea Islands and was one of the first black military units formed by the Lincoln administration.

Like all of the black regiments, the First South Carolina Volunteers desperately needed medical assistance. Susie was working as a laundress for her husband's company. Although she had no formal training, she quickly offered her services and became the first black army nurse to serve her country. Later, other black women joined the troops to nurse their men, including Harriet Tubman and Sojourner Truth. But Susie is believed to be the first. In addition to nursing the soldiers, Susie also took the time to teach the men how to read and write.

Edward King died at the end of the Civil War and Susie moved north to Boston. There she met and married Russell Taylor in 1879. Susie had worked as a volunteer nurse on the battlefront for four years, tending the wounded soldiers. For her heroism and dedication to her people and her country Susie received no pay and no pension. In 1902, Susie published her memoirs, *My Life in Camp with the 33rd United States Colored Troops.*

Bessie Coleman

Aviatrix
1893–1926
Birthplace: Atlanta, Texas

If I can create the minimum of my plans and desires, there shall be no regrets.

When Bessie was seven years old, her father, who was part African and part Native American, returned to Oklahoma Indian Territory, leaving her mother behind to raise the family alone. As a result, Bessie's life as a child was hard. She picked cotton and helped her mother do laundry to make money for family expenses. Unable to find satisfactory work after graduation from high school, Bessie left Texas and joined her brother in Chicago to make a better life for herself.

There she trained as a manicurist and took a job at a barber shop. Still not satisfied with her life, Bessie became interested in flying airplanes and tried to enroll in aviation schools. But because she was black and a woman, she was turned down. She sought the advice of a friend, newspaper editor Robert Abbott, who told Bessie that she should go to flying school in Europe where she would not face such prejudice. With his help, Bessie studied French, saved her money, and sailed to France.

After making two trips to Europe, and studying with French and German aviators, Bessie became the first black woman in the world to receive an international pilot's license. Upon her return to Chicago, Bessie started a new career—exhibition flying.

Her first show was in 1922 at Chicago's Checkerboard Field. Crowds of spectators turned out to witness the stunts of the brave, 29-year-old black woman. Bessie did not disappoint them. Her plane dipped and twirled, made loops and figure eights, and the audience was thrilled.

Bessie continued to perform in air shows all across the country for the next four years. After seeing her, many young African Americans were eager to learn how to fly. Many contacted Bessie for help. Bessie dreamed of having her own flying school for African Americans one day and began planning for it. She died, however, in an airplane crash during a test flight before that dream could be realized.

Bessie would be pleased to know that an organization of young black women pilots has been named in her honor. The goal of the Bessie Coleman Aviators is to bring the thrill of flight to all black and other women of color interested in aviation and aerospace.

Jane C. Wright

Cancer Research Specialist
1919–
Birthplace: New York, New York

There is deep satisfaction in knowing you are part of a continuing process and program and that you have picked up where others have left off and that others will pick up where you leave off.

A s a little girl, Jane Wright had big footsteps in which to follow. Her father, Louis Tompkins Wright, was one of the country's outstanding surgeons and medical researchers. He was also an important force in the civil rights movement and served as chairman of the National Board of Directors of the NAACP. Sometimes having a famous parent is difficult for a child. This was not the case with Jane. Her father's outstanding career was an inspiration to her. She was motivated to excel.

Three years after graduating from New York Medical College in 1945, Jane joined the Harlem Hospital Cancer Research Foundation, which her father had founded. There she worked as a clinician. After her father's death in 1952, Jane succeeded him as director of the foundation. She concentrated her efforts on research, studying the effects of chemotherapy on tumors and other abnormal growths.

In 1955, Jane was named director of cancer chemotherapy and adjunct associate professor of research surgery at New York University School of Medicine. Then in 1967, she was appointed associate dean and professor of surgery at New York Medical College, the highest position ever held by an African-American woman in medical administration.

Jane has published 124 scientific papers and has written chapters for nine textbooks on cancer and cancer research. In 1975, the American Association for Cancer Research honored Jane for her important contributions to research in clinical cancer chemotherapy.

Although Jane is retired, she still leads an active life. She is professor emeritus of surgery at New York Medical College. In 1983, Jane was featured in a Smithsonian Institute series exhibit titled, "Black Women: Achievements Against the Odds." She is currently compiling papers about her work for a collection at Smith College. Like her father, Jane has become a role model for other young African-American scientists and doctors.

Jewel Plummer Cobb

Biologist and Educator
1924–
Birthplace: Chicago, Illinois

I am angry at the condition of society that creates problems for blacks and women. But I think there are ways anger can be turned into something positive.

J ewel comes from a family of doctors and Ph.D.'s. Her father had a medical practice in Chicago, where he cared for other African Americans. Jewel is a third-generation doctor and her son, a radiologist, is the fourth.

Despite being surrounded by doctors and science, Jewel was a sophomore in high school when she looked through a microscope in laboratory and decided then that biology was for her. After graduating from high school, she attended the University of Michigan, but she left because black students were not allowed to live in the dormitories. This was in 1941. So she transferred to Talladega, a black college, and graduated in 1944.

After receiving her doctorate degree in cell biology from New York University in 1950, Jewel did cancer research. She wrote over 36 papers and performed extensive studies of cell biology with the hope of finding some clue to the treatment of cancer. Jewel became very well known as a prominent cancer researcher.

During her career, Jewel has held many faculty and administrative positions at various universities, including deanships at Connecticut College and Douglass College at Rutgers University. All the while, she continued to conduct research. In 1981, she was named president of California State University at Fullerton, which serves 22,000 students. With that appointment, Jewel became one of the few African-American women to head a college or university.

Jewel is currently serving as President Emeritus, California State University, Fullerton, and as Trustee Professor, California State University, Los Angeles. But despite her success as an administrator and educator, Jewel still considers herself, first and foremost, a biologist.

Jewel is worried, however, that more African-American students are not going into science. "When I see more black students in the laboratories than I see on the football field," she has said, "then I'll be happy."

Clarice D. Reid

Director, Sickle Cell Program
National Institutes of Health
1931–
Birthplace: Birmingham, Alabama

I still have much more to achieve. If I had
already achieved it all, I'd go home and sew!

Sickle-cell anemia is a disease of the blood that occurs primarily in people of African descent. It affects one out of five hundred black babies born in the United States. Victims of the disease suffer great pain, infections, and strokes. They often die young, and as yet, there is no known cure.

Since the disease was discovered here in the United States in 1910, doctors from all over the world have been searching for a cure. Until one is found, all they can hope to do is help sickle-cell sufferers live with the disease.

Dr. Clarice Reid is one of these doctors. She was always interested in the health problems of minorities. In medical school—where she was the only black student—she specialized in pediatrics and family medicine. This allowed her to learn about all the diseases that affect children and their families. After graduating from the University of Cincinnati Medical School in 1959, Dr. Reid became the only African-American pediatrician in private practice in Cincinnati, Ohio.

Meanwhile, a lot of exciting research was being done in the area of sickle-cell anemia at Howard University in Washington, D.C. Dr. Reid went to Washington, and her interest in helping sickle-cell patients grew. As the deputy director of the Sickle Cell Program of the Health Service Administration, Dr. Reid helped to make people aware of the disease, particularly African Americans. She developed a national program to reduce the death rate from the disease and has taught nurses, social workers, and other health professionals how to care for sickle-cell patients.

Because of Clarice Reid's work, the care for sickle-cell patients in the past 15 years has improved greatly. The life span and the quality of life for these patients has been much improved as well.

Dr. Reid has received many honors for her work, including the Public Health Service Superior Service Award, which is the highest honor given by the United States Public Health Service.

Faye Wattleton

Protector of Women's Reproductive Rights
1943–
Birthplace: St. Louis, Missouri

To be able to take control of their reproductive lives was perhaps more liberating than any other advancement that women have achieved.

When Faye Wattleton was a child, African Americans in many parts of the United States were not allowed to use the same bathrooms as whites. So when black families drove through the country, they would ask the gas station attendant if there were bathroom facilities for blacks before they bought gas. Faye remembers one instance when her family was told that, yes, there was a "colored" bathroom. But when Faye went to find it, she found only an open hole in the ground. "My father protested," she said, "and he said, 'We're not dogs. Stop pumping the gas.' In Algiers, Louisiana, that could have been reason for lynching."

The strength of mind and moral courage that her father displayed also characterizes Faye. She holds a nursing degree, a master's degree in maternal and infant care, and is certified as a nurse-midwife. Early in her career, when she worked as a nurse in New York City's Harlem Hospital, Faye witnessed firsthand the desperation and suffering of women who had unintended pregnancies and illegal, unsafe abortions. She became determined to help all women—especially the poor and the young—gain access to the full range of reproductive health options available to them.

Planned Parenthood Federation of America is the country's oldest and largest voluntary reproductive health organization. It is dedicated to the principle that every individual has a fundamental right to choose when to have children.

Faye became very active in this organization and was made the executive director of the Planned Parenthood affiliate in Dayton, Ohio. From 1978-1992, Faye served as president of the national organization, headquartered in New York City. Under her leadership, Planned Parenthood now plays a major role in shaping the family-planning policies of America and of governments worldwide. Faye has received many honorary doctorate degrees and awards for her work.

"My mother felt that I should be a missionary nurse," she has said, "I think, from my own view, I have done missionary work nonetheless."

Mae C. Jemison

First Black Female Astronaut
1956–
Birthplace: Decatur, Alabama

The most important challenge in my life is to always test the limits of my abilities, do the best job I can at the time while remaining true to myself.

In August 1987, Dr. Mae Jemison was sitting at her desk at a hospital in Los Angeles. She was between patients, taking care of some paperwork, when the phone rang. It was a representative of the National Aeronautics and Space Administration (NASA). The young physician was told she had been chosen as an astronaut candidate. She could become the first African-American woman to travel in space.

This was just the latest in a series of notable accomplishments by the multitalented Mae Jemison. Born in Alabama but raised in Chicago, Mae received her bachelor of science degree in chemical engineering and a bachelor of arts degree in African and Afro-American Studies simultaneously at Stanford University. From there she enrolled in Cornell University Medical College where she became very active in student and community-based groups. She also maintained her interest in Third World countries. Mae travelled to Cuba, Kenya, and Thailand to work and continue her medical training.

After graduating from medical school, Mae joined the Peace Corps and worked in Africa supervising health-care programs for Peace Corps personnel. Upon her return, she worked as a general practitioner in Los Angeles. She then applied for admission to the astronaut program.

Three months after Mae first applied to NASA, the *Challenger* disaster occurred, taking the lives of seven astronauts, including that of an African American, Ronald McNair. But the incident did not deter Mae. She simply reapplied when the selection process was reopened. A year later, she was notified that she had been chosen from nearly 2,000 applicants as one of the 15 members of NASA's 1987 astronaut-training program.

Mae completed a one-year training and evaluation program in August 1988. Mae is the world's first black female astronaut. She travelled into space in August 1992, on Space Lab J. This mission was a cooperative venture between the United States and Japan and focused on research in life sciences and material development.

CHRONOLOGY

DATE	EVENT

1500s   **The British, Dutch, Spanish, and Portuguese begin trafficking African people in the brutal European slave trade.**

1600s   Queen Nzingha of Angola fights the Portuguese and the enslavement of her people.

1619   **The first boatload of Africans arrives in Virginia.** The institution of slavery is firmly established in the American colonies.

1660   The number of American slaves increases rapidly as the British gain control over much of the slave trade.

1770   Phillis Wheatley publishes her first poem, becoming the earliest known published African-American woman writer.

1775   **The American Revolution begins.** The 13 American colonies fight for their independence from British rule. One of the first casualties of the war is a black man, Crispus Attucks.

1776   **Congress adopts the Declaration of Independence and creates the United States of America.** Although based on the theory of natural rights, the Declaration of Independence does not extend these rights to African Americans.

1783   The Treaty of Paris recognizes the United States as a nation, ending the American Revolution.

1793   **The Fugitive Slave Act is passed.** This law makes harboring a slave a criminal offense.

1807   Britain outlaws the slave trade and later abolishes slavery in the British Empire (1833), but American slaveholders continue to keep one million African-American slaves under their control to work the plantations of the Southern states.

1839   Joseph Cinque and other captured Africans take over the slave ship *Amistad*, demanding to be returned to Africa. They are ultimately set free by a U.S. Supreme Court decision in 1841.

1843   Sojourner Truth starts her own campaign against slavery.

1846   Harriet Tubman escapes slavery and begins conducting on the Underground Railroad.

Poet Frances Watkins Harper speaks out against slavery, traveling throughout the South.

1848   **The right of women to vote is proposed for the first time** by women's rights leaders Elizabeth Cady Stanton and Lucretia Mott.

1850   **The Underground Railroad is fully functioning,** helping Southern slaves escape to the North and to Canada. Mary Ellen and William Craft are two of the Railroad's "passengers." Sculptor Edmonia Lewis is one of many abolitionist friends along the Railroad's "track."

1856   After being taken from Mississippi to California by her master, Biddy Mason gains her freedom. She becomes a wealthy landowner, one of the first black women in Los Angeles to own property.

1857   **In the Dred Scott decision, the U.S. Supreme Court denies citizenship rights to blacks,** opens federal territory to slavery, and decrees that slaves are not free just because they are taken into free territory.

1861	**The Civil War begins** between the North and South. Many slaves flee to the South Carolina Sea Islands. There Charlotte Forten Grimké teaches freedmen how to read and write.

1861   **The Civil War begins** between the North and South. Many slaves flee to the South Carolina Sea Islands. There Charlotte Forten Grimké teaches freedmen how to read and write.

1863   **President Abraham Lincoln signs the Emancipation Proclamation granting freedom to all slaves.**

1864   Rebecca Cole and Rebecca Lee are the first two African-American women in the United States to receive medical degrees.

1865   **The Civil War ends.** African Americans begin to exercise their voting rights and to function as citizens in American society as Black Reconstruction begins. Fannie Jackson Coppin starts teaching at the Institute for Colored Youth (now called Cheyney University) in Philadelphia.

1872   In the mid-19th century, African Americans start to win recognition as lawyers. Charlotte E. Ray becomes the first black woman to receive a law degree in the United States.

1891   Ida B. Wells starts her lifelong antilynching campaign by establishing her own newspaper, the *Memphis Free Speech*, to draw attention to the brutal lynch mob murders of black Americans.

1896   Mary Church Terrell is elected president of the National Association of Colored Women.

       In *Plessy v. Ferguson*, the U.S. Supreme Court upholds legal segregation.

1899   Mary Eliza Mahoney is the first African-American woman to graduate from a professional white nursing school.

1903   Maggie Lena Walker establishes the St. Luke Penny Savings Bank, which becomes the St. Luke Bank and Trust Company. She becomes America's first woman bank president.

1904   After teaching at Haines Institute (founded by Lucy Craft Laney), Mary McLeod Bethune establishes a school now known as Bethune-Cookman College.

1909   **National Association for the Advancement of Colored People (NAACP) is formed.** Ida B. Wells and Mary Terrell are founding members.

1910   Madame C.J. Walker opens her own beauty care factory. She goes on to become America's first black millionaire, a philanthropist, and supporter of black artists in Harlem.

       The first case of sickle-cell anemia is identified in the United States.

1911   **The Universal Negro Improvement Association (UNIA) is formed by Marcus Garvey.** Garvey forms and popularizes the "Back to Africa" movement.

1914   **World War I begins.** Almost 400,000 African-American men serve in the armed forces, mostly in service units. The 92nd and 93rd all-black infantry divisions, however, prove to be outstanding fighting forces.

       The great migration of African Americans from the rural South to the cities of the industrial North is underway. New York City's Harlem becomes a key urban center in the Northeast.

1915   *Birth of a Nation*, a blatantly racist film, is released across the country to a storm of protest by the NAACP and the black community. The humiliating images of African Americans are propaganda, but are accepted by many as real. Violence against blacks increases as a result of this film.

1920s   **The Nineteenth Amendment to the Constitution guarantees women the right to vote.**

       The Harlem Rennaissance is at its height. Writers such as Zora Neale Hurston, Arna Bontemps, Jessie Fauset, Claude McKay, Jean Toomer, and Langston Hughes produce some of their greatest works during this period.

1922	Bessie Coleman, the first black American female pilot, performs her first air show in Chicago.
1929	**The Great Depression begins.**
1933	Lena Horne joins the chorus line of Harlem's famous Cotton Club. This is the beginning of her legendary performing career.
1935	**The National Council of Negro Women is formed.** Mary McLeod Bethune is the founder.
1938	Ella Fitzgerald records "A-Tisket, A-Tasket," and becomes "The First Lady of Song."
1939	**World War II breaks out in Europe.** Over one million African Americans serve, including several thousand women. Despite the proven abilities of African-American troops, the units are still segregated until the end of the war.
	Actress Hattie McDaniel becomes the first African American to win an Academy Award, and singer Marian Anderson performs on the steps of the Lincoln Memorial at the request of Eleanor Roosevelt. Augusta Savage's famous sculpture, *Lift Every Voice and Sing*, is unveiled at the New York World's Fair.
1945	**World War II ends.**
1946	Gospel singer Mahalia Jackson records "Move on Up a Little Higher" and becomes internationally famous.
1948	Alice Coachman becomes the first black American woman to win a gold medal in the high jump in the Olympic Games.
	The racist system of apartheid is formalized in South Africa.
1950	Althea Gibson breaks new ground when she plays the U.S. Open tennis competition, becoming the first African American ever to do so.
	Attorney Edith Sampson becomes the first African American to serve as a delegate to the United Nations.
	For her book of poetry, *Annie Allen*, Gwendolyn Brooks becomes the first African American to win a Pulitzer Prize.
1954	**In *Brown v. Board of Education of Topeka, Kansas*, the U.S. Supreme Court reverses the "separate but equal" doctrine of *Plessy v. Ferguson*.**
1955	Rosa Parks refuses to give up her seat on a **Montgomery** bus to a white man. The incident sparks a **381-day bus boycott** lead by Dr. Martin Luther King, Jr.
1956	South African singer Miriam Makeba tours the world, spreading the truth about apartheid. As a result, she is exiled from her country.
1957	Despite threats to their lives, Daisy Bates and the Little Rock Nine successfully integrate Central High School in Little Rock, Arkansas.
1958	Alvin Ailey founds the Alvin Ailey American Dance Theater. Judith Jamison joins the troupe eight years later, and becomes its artistic director in 1989 after Ailey's death.
1959	Martin Luther King, Jr. organizes the **Southern Christian Leadership Conference** with other black leaders. Activist Ella Baker plays a major role in its formation; she later helps organize the **Student Non-Violent Coordinating Committee.** Educator Septima Clark sets up Freedom Schools all over the South.
	Lorraine Hansberry's *A Raisin in the Sun* opens on Broadway and wins the New York Drama Critics Circle Award.
1961	**Freedom Rides begin.**
	Opera singer Leontyne Price makes her Metropolitan Opera House debut singing *Il Trovatore*.

1962	South African lawyer and civil rights leader Nelson Mandela receives life imprisonment for an act of treason against the South African government. Despite police harassment, his wife, Winnie Mandela, continues to speak out against apartheid and to fight for Nelson's release and the freedom of her people.
1963	A Birmingham church is bombed, killing four black children.
	Two hundred and fifty thousand people demonstrate at the historic March on Washington in support of the passage of the Civil Rights Act, which outlaws segregation and ensures voter rights and protection. At the march, Martin Luther King, Jr. gives his famous "I Have a Dream" speech.
	Civil rights leader Medgar Evers is assassinated.
1964	**The Civil Rights Act passes.** Constance Baker Motley is elected to the New York State Senate, the first black woman to sit in the senate in that state's history.
	Martin Luther King, Jr. is awarded the Nobel Peace Prize.
1965	Because of the enthusiasm and activism on the part of many African Americans—like Fannie Lou Hamer, a sharecropper who simply wanted to vote—the **Voting Rights Act of 1965 is passed.** It provides for federal examination of voter registration procedures and gives the U.S. Attorney General the authority to sue a principality on behalf of persons deprived of their right to vote.
	Human rights leader Malcolm X is assassinated.
1967	Aretha Franklin's song "Respect" is released and becomes a phenomenal success. Rhythm and blues ("soul music") finally becomes acceptable and popular with whites and blacks alike. Up until the late 1950s, black music was not allowed to be played on white radio stations.
1968	**Martin Luther King, Jr. is assassinated.** Coretta Scott King continues to spread his message.
	Shirley Chisholm is elected the first African-American congresswoman.
1972	Shirley Chisholm becomes the first African-American woman to make a bid for the nomination for the presidency of the United States.
1973	Clara McBride Hale founds Hale House to care for drug-addicted babies. She is later named an "American Hero" by President Ronald Reagan in 1985.
	In *Roe v. Wade,* the U.S. Supreme Court rules that states may not ban abortions and that the 14th amendment protects a woman from state intrusion into her decision as to whether or not to bear a child.
1974	Cicely Tyson is nominated for an Academy Award for her role in *Sounder.* Later she wins an Emmy Award for her performance as Jane Pittman in "The Autobiography of Miss Jane Pittman."
1983	Alice Walker wins a Pulitzer Prize for her novel, *The Color Purple.*
1986	Dorothy Height of the National Council of Negro Women founds the annual Black Family Reunion Celebration.
1988	Jesse Jackson runs for the Democratic nomination for president of the United States.
	Toni Morrison wins a Pulitzer Prize for her novel, *Beloved.*
1990	Under pressure by the world's leaders, South Africa begins dismantling some of its apartheid practices.
	Nelson Mandela is released from prison in South Africa.
	Miriam Makeba returns home to South Africa after years of exile.

SELECTED BIBLIOGRAPHY

Aaseng, Nathan, *Florence Griffith Joyner: Dazzling Olympian*, Minneapolis: Lerner, 1989 *(gr. 4–9)*

Bell, Roseanne P.; Parker, Bettye J.; and Guy-Sheftall, Beverley; ed. *Sturdy Black Bridges: Visions of Black Women in Literature*, Garden City: Anchor, 1979

Bentley, Judith, *Harriet Tubman*, New York: F. Watts, 1990 *(YA)*

Bogle, Donald, *Brown Sugar: Eighty Years of America's Black Female Superstars*, New York: Harmony Books, 1980

Brown, Cynthia S., *Ready from Within: Septima Clark and the Civil Rights Movement*, Trenton: Africa World Press, Inc, 1990

Freedman, Florence B., *Two Tickets to Freedom: The True Story of Ellen and William Craft, Fugitive Slaves*, New York: Peter Bedrick Books, 1989 *(gr. 4 up)*

Giddins, Paula, *When and Where I Enter: The Impact of Black Women on Race and Sex in America*, New York: William Morrow, 1984

Green, Richard L., ed., *A Salute to Historic Black Women*, Chicago: Empak Publishing, 1988

Haber, Louis, *Black Pioneers of Science and Invention*, San Diego: Harcourt Brace Jovanovich, 1987

Halasa, Malu, *Mary McLeod Bethune*, Black Americans of Achievement Series, New York: Chelsea House Publishers, 1989 *(gr. 5 up)*

Haskins, James, *Black Music in America: A History Through Its People*, New York: Crowell Junior Books, 1987 *(gr. 7 up)*

Haskins, James, *Winnie Mandela: Life of Struggle*, New York: Putnam, 1988 *(gr. 6 up)*

Hudson, Wade and Wesley, Valerie Wilson, *AFRO-BETS Book of Black Heroes From A to Z*, Orange, NJ: Just Us Books, 1988 *(gr. 4 up)*

Hull, Gloria, Scott, Patricia Bell and Smith, Barbara, editors, *But Some of Us Are Brave: Black Women's Studies*, New York: The Feminist Press, 1982

Jackson, Carlton, *Hattie: The Life of Hattie McDaniel*, Lanham, Maryland: Madison Books, 1990

Jensen, Marilyn, *Phillis Wheatley: Negro Slave*, Batavia, Illinois: Lion, 1987 *(gr. 5–9)*

Kranz, Rachel, *Biographical Dictionary of Black Americans*, New York: Facts on File, 1989 *(YA)*

Kuklin, Susan, *Reaching for Dreams: A Ballet from Rehearsal to Opening Night* (The Alvin Ailey Dance Theater), New York: Lothrop, Lee & Shepard, 1987 *(gr. 4–9)*

Lerner, Gerda, ed. *Black Women in White America: A Documentary History*, New York: Vintage, 1972

Levine, Ellen, *If You Traveled on the Underground Railroad*, New York: Scholastic, 1988 *(gr. 4–6)*

Lewis, Mary C, *Herstory, Black Female Rites of Passage*, Chicago: African American Images, 1988 *(YA)*

McKissack, Patricia and Fredrick, *The Civil Rights Movement in America from 1865 to the Present*, Chicago: Childrens Press, 1987 *(gr. 4–5)*

McKissack, Patricia, *Mary McLeod Bethune: A Great American Educator*, People of Distinction Series, Chicago: Childrens Press, 1985 *(gr. 5–8)*

Moore, Mafori; Gilyard, Gwen Akua; King, Karen; and Warfield-Coppock, Nsenga, *Transformation: A Rites of Passage Manual for African American Girls*, New York: STARS Press, 1987 *(YA)*

Moutoussamy-Ashe, Jeanne, *Viewfinders, Black Women Photographers*, New York: Dodd Mead, 1986

Noble, Jeanne, *Beautiful Also, Are the Souls of My Black Sisters: A History of the Black Woman in America*, Englewood Cliffs: Prentice-Hall, 1978

Patrick, Diane, *Coretta Scott King*, New York: F. Watts, 1990 *(gr. 4–9)*

Pelz, Ruth, *Black Heroes of the Wild West*, Seattle: Open Hand Publishing, 1989 *(gr. 5–8)*

Petry, Ann, *Harriet Tubman: Conductor on the Underground Railroad*, New York: Pocket Books, 1955

Robinson, Jo Ann Gibson, with Garrow, David J., ed., *The Montgomery Bus Boycott and the Women Who Started It: The Memoir of Jo Ann Gibson Robinson*, Knoxville: The University of Tennessee Press, 1987

Sterling, Dorothy, *Black Foremothers*, New York: The Feminist Press, 1988

Sterling, Dorothy, *We Are Your Sisters: Black Women in the Nineteenth Century*, New York: W. W. Norton & Company, 1984

Taylor-Bond, Susan, *Sojourner Truth*, Wilton, Connecticut: Morehouse, 1990 *(gr. 5–6)*

Tessendorf, K.C., *Along the Road to Soweto: A Racial History of South Africa*, New York: Atheneum, 1989 *(gr. 6 up)*

Witcover, Paul, *Zora Neale Hurston*, New York: Chelsea House, 1991 *(gr. 6–12)*

SOURCE NOTES

Sources of italicized quoted material reprinted within this volume are indicated below according to the page on which each quote appears. Every effort has been made to trace the ownership of all copyrighted material and to secure the necessary permissions to reprint each selection. In the event of any question arising as to the fair use of any material or any inadvertent error, the publisher will be happy to make the necessary correction in future printings. Thanks are gratefully extended to individuals and publishers for permission to reprint copyrighted materials.

3 "I Am A Black Woman," copyright by Mari Evans. Extract reprinted from the poem, "I Am A Black Woman" by permission of the author.

4 Sojourner Truth, from a speech at the 1852 Women's Rights Convention, Akron, Ohio.

5 Van Sertima, Ivan, Great *Black Leaders: Ancient and Modern* © 1988 by Journal of African Civilizations, Ltd., Inc.

6 H*istoric Negro Biographies, Vol. 4 of International Library of Negro Life and History*

7 Ibid

8 Lerner, Gerda, *Black Women in White America: A Documentary History* © 1972 Vintage Books, a Division of Random House, NY.

9 Sterling, Dorothy, B*lack Foremothers: Three Lives*, © 1988 The Feminist Press at the City University of New York.

10 Duster, Alfreda M., C*rusade for Justice: The Autobiography of Ida B. Wells* © 1970 U. of Chicago Press, Chicago, IL.

11 Essence, February 1990, "Amy-Jacques Garvey: On the Front Lines," by Jean Wiley.

12 White, Joyce. "A Witness to the History," New York Daily News, Feb. 3, 1985 p. 3.

13 Lerner, Bla*ck Women in White America*, op. cit.

14 Lanker, Brian, I *Dream a World: Portraits of Black Women Who Changed America*, © 1989, Stewart, Tabori and Chang, Inc. New York, NY.

15 Ebony, August 1990, "Has the New Generation Changed the Civil Rights Agenda?" Ebony Special Edition: "The New Generation of the 90s," Johnson Publishing Co., Chicago, IL.

16 Lanker, I *Dream a World*, op. cit.

17 Lerner, *Black Women in White America*, op. cit.

18 Lanker, I *Dream a World*, op. cit.

19 Mandela, Winnie, P*art of My Soul Went with Him*, © 1985 W. W. Norton & Company, NY.

20 Lanker, I *Dream a World*, op. cit.

21 Essence, August, 1986 "Angela Davis, Talking Tough" by Cheryl Y. Greene.

22 Poetry extract courtesy of Marva Collins, author.

23 Lerner, Bla*ck Women in White America*, op. cit.

Sterling, Dorothy, W*e Are your Sisters: Black Women in the Nineteenth Century*, © 1984 W. W. Norton & Company, NY.

25 A *Salute to Historic Black Educators*, an Empak "Black History" Publication, © 1984 Chicago, IL.

26 Bethune, Mary McLeod, "Faith That Moved a Dump Heap," Who, The Magazine About People. Vol 1 No. 3 June 1941.

27 Clark, Septima, *Ready From Within* © 1986 edited by Cynthia Stokes Brown, Africa World Press, Trenton, NJ.

28 Lanker, I *Dream a World*, op. cit.

29 Schomburg clipping file

30 Lanker, I *Dream a World*, op. cit.

31 personal interview with Mary Futrell

32 Angelou, Maya, "And Still I Rise" excerpt © 1977 Maya Angelou, And *Still I Rise*, Random House, NY. Reprinted by permission of the author.

33 Wheatley, Phillis, *The Poems of Phillis Wheatley* by Julian Nelson, ed. © 1989, The University of North Carolina Press.

34 Harper, Frances, I*ola Leroy: Shadows Uplifted*, reprinted 1988, Oxford University Press, NYC.

35 Katz, William Loren, *The Black West*, © 1987 by Ethrac Publications, Inc. Open Hand Publishing Inc. Seattle, WA.

36 Kellner, Bruce, ed. *The Harlem Renaissance: A Historical Dictionary for the Era*, © 1984 Greenwood Press, Westport, Conn.

37 Hurston, Zora Neale, *Their Eyes Were Watching God* © 1937, renewed 1965. Reprinted by permission of Harper & Row Publishers Inc., NY.

38 *Current Biographies*, The H. W. Wilson Company, NY.

39 Metzger, Linda et al., *Black Writers: A Selection of Sketches from Contemporary Authors*, © 1989 Gale Research, Inc., Detroit MI.

40 Ibid

41 Lanker, I *Dream a World*, op. cit.

42 Lansberry, Lorraine, T*o Be Young Gifted and Black in Her Own Words*, adapted by Robert Nemiroff, © 1969 Reprinted by permission of Prentice-Hall, Inc., Englewood Cliffs, NJ.

43 Metzger, Linda, B*lack Writers*, op. cit.

44 *Current Biographies*, The H. W. Wilson Company, NY.

45 Lorna Simpson exhibit brochure from the Museum of Modern Art, 1990.

46 Makeba, Miriam, with James Hall, M*akeba: My Story* © 1987, New American Library, NY.

47 Null, Gary, *Black Hollywood: The Negro in Motion Pictures*, © 1975 Citadel Press, NJ.

48 Lanker, I *Dream a World*, op. cit.

49 Berendt, Joachim E., *The Jazz Book: From Ragtime to Fusion and Beyond*, © 1982 Lawrence Hill & Company, Conn.

50 Lanker, I *Dream a World*, op. cit.

51 Jackson, Mahalia, *Movin' On Up*, © 1966 Hawthorn Books, Inc. NY.

52 Lanker, I *Dream a World*, op. cit.

53 Fitzgerald, Ella. *Contributions of Black Women in America*.

54 Lanker, I *Dream A World*, op. cit.

55 Lanker, _____

56 Lanker, _____

57 Makeba, Miriam, *My Story*, op. cit.

59 Lanker, I *Dream a World*, op. cit.

60 *Current Biographies*, The H. W. Wilson Company. NY.

61 Ad Supplement to Essence, December 1990

62 Lanker, I *Dream a World*, op. cit.

64 Lanker, _____

65 Lanker, _____

66 Aaseng, Nathan, *Florence Griffith Joyner*, © 1989 Lerner Publications, Minneapolis, MN.

67 "Cheryl Miller Sets Model for Area Girls", Cincinnati Enquirer, November 29, 1986.

68 Lanker, I *Dream a World*, op. cit.

69 Hayden, Dolores, "Biddy Mason's Los Angeles, 1856-1891." California History, Fall 1989 p. 99.

70 Schomburg picture file, Speech from National Negro Business League, 1912 Convention.

71 Daniel, Sadie Iola, *Women Builders*, © 1931 The Associated Publishers, Inc. Washington DC.

72 Susan Taylor, "In the Spirit," Essence, October 1990.

73 Ms. January, 1986, "Suzanne de Passe" by Rosemary Bray.

74 Black Enterprise, August 1986, "Child's Play" by Jube Silver.

75 Lanker, I *Dream a World*, op. cit.

76 Lanker, _____

77 *Howard University President's Report*, 1870

78 *Current Biography, 1950* ed. Anna Roth, The W. W. Wilson Company, c 1951 NY.

79 Lerner, *Black Women in White America*, op. cit.

80 Lanker, I *Dream a World*, op. cit.

81 Ebony, November 1990, "What's Ahead for Black and Whites 45 Years From Today?" by Cardiss Collins. © Johnson Publishing Company, Chicago, IL.

82 Lanker, I *Dream a World*, op. cit.

83 *Current Biographies*, The H. W. Wilson Company, NY.

84 Lanker, I *Dream a World*, op. cit.

85 Ms., January 1984, "A Day in the Life of Maxine Waters," by Beverly Beyette.

86 Publisher's correspondence with Mae Jemison.

87 from publication of the American Nurses's Association

88 Sterling, *We Are Your Sisters*, op. cit.

89 Lerner, *Black Women in White America*, op. cit.

90 Ebony, May 1977, "They Take to the Sky". Johnson Publishing Company, Chicago, IL.

91 press release reprint of *Images* Magazine, Fall 1988, New York Medical College, Valhalla, NY.

92 Lanker, I *Dream a World*, op. cit.

93 Black Enterprise, October 1988, "Seeking New Blood to Stop Sickle Cell."

94 Lanker, I *Dream A World*, op. cit.

95 Publisher's correspondence with Mae Jemison

ABOUT THE AUTHORS

TOYOMI IGUS

A veteran of the West Coast magazine publishing industry, Toyomi Igus is currently managing editor of UCLA's Center for Afro-American Studies Publications where she edits and produces books and journals about the African-American experience. She is also the executive editor of the *ABBWA Journal*, a magazine that focuses on blacks in publishing. Toyomi's first picture book for children, *When I Was Little*, was published by Just Us Books in 1992.

VERONICA FREEMAN ELLIS

Veronica Freeman Ellis is the author of *Land of the Four Winds*, published by Just Us Books. A former textbook editor, Veronica currently teaches writing at Boston University and children's literature at Wheelock College, Boston. She is also a consultant/instructor for the Davis Educational Foundation's Children's Literature In-Service Program. Veronica is working on several books for children about her country, Liberia.

DIANE PATRICK

Diane Patrick's books for young readers include *Martin Luther King, Jr.* and *Coretta Scott King*, both published by Franklin Watts. Her articles for young readers have appeared in *Harambee*, a newspaper for young readers that focuses on the African American experience. Diane has also written for a number of music magazines, including *Billboard*, *Jazziz*, *JazzTimes*, and *Wire* (U.K.). A former paralegal, Diane also contributes to *Legal Assistant Today*.

VALERIE WILSON WESLEY

Valerie Wesley is currently the executive editor of *Essence* magazine. She is also co-author of *AFRO-BETS Book of Black Heroes From A to Z*, published by Just Us Books. The title has over 100,000 copies in print. Valerie's stories and articles for children and young adults have appeared in *Essence, Choices, Creative Classroom,* and *Scholastic News.* She is presently working on a young adult novel.

ACKNOWLEDGMENTS We would like to thank the following people for their valuable assistance in reviewing and/or preparing material for this book: Shanda Barnett; Marquita Guerra, Marron Publishers; Wade Hudson; Anna Marie Muskelly; Barbara Omolade; Barbara Smith, Kitchen Table: Women of Color Press.

Photo Credits are listed by page number and source as follows:

Schomburg Center for Research in Black Culture, New York:
4, 5, 7, 9, 10, 11, 13, 17, 24, 26, 28, 29, 32, 33, 34, 36, 37, 42, 49, 52, 55, 58, 59, 65, 70, 71, 80, 87, 89, 90. Also cover photos of Rosa Parks and Bessie Coleman.

Page 6, National Portrait Gallery/Smithsonian Institute, Washington, DC; 8, taken from William Still's *Underground Railroad;* 12, © E. Lee White, photographer; 14 and cover photo; courtesy of Hale House, 15, National Council of Negro Women, Washington DC; 16, courtesy of Rosa Parks Institute, Detroit MI; 18, Martin Luther King Center for Non-Violent Social Change, Inc., Atlanta, GA; 19, W. W. Norton & Company Inc., NY; 20, Children's Defense Fund, Washington, DC; 21, © Orlanda Uffre, photographer; 22 and 30, courtesy of Westside Preparatory School, Chicago, IL; 23, private collection; 25, Georgia Dept. of Archives and History, Atlanta, GA; 27, courtesy of Highlander Center, New Market, TN; 31, courtesy of Mary Futrell; 32, © Marvin/Morgan Smith; 35, courtesy of Boston Athenaeum; 38, courtesy of Margaret Walker; 39, Third World Press, Chicago, IL; 40, courtesy of Putnam & Grosset Group, © Jerry Bauer, photographer; 41, courtesy of Maya Angelou; 43, courtesy of Knopf © Maia Mulas, photographer; 44, courtesy of Harcourt, Brace, Javonovich, © Jeff Reinking, Picture Group; 45, courtesy of Josh Baer Gallery © Stephen Chin, photographer; 46, Alvin Ailey American Dance Theater, NY © Max Waldman; 47, 50, and 53, AP/Wide World Photos, Inc.; 48, Granger Collection; 51 and 78, courtesy of Estate of Carl Van Vechten, Joseph Solomon, executor/print from Yale Collection of American Literature, Beineke Library, Yale University; 54, Henry Holt and Company, Inc., NY; 56, courtesy of Winnie Klotz, Metropolitan Opera, NY; 60, Arista, © Norman Parkinson; 61, Alvin Ailey American Dance Theater, © Michael Ahearn, photographer; 62, 63, 66, AP/Wide World Photos, Inc.; 64, Bettman, NY; 67, courtesy of ABC © Capital Cities/ABC Inc.; 68 and 75, courtesy of Harpo Productions, Inc., Chicago, IL; 72, courtesy of Essence magazine, NY; 73, Gordy/dePasse Productions, Los Angeles, CA; 74, courtesy of NBC Entertainment, Burbank, CA; 76 and 79, AP/Wide World Photos, Inc.; 81, 84, and 85, courtesy of U.S. House of Representatives; 82, courtesy of Jones, Day, Reavis & Pogue, Los Angeles, CA; 83, courtesy of University of Texas, Austin; 86 and 95, courtesy of NASA; 91, copyright Smith College Archives, photo by Dick Fish; 92, courtesy of California State University, Los Angeles; 93, courtesy of Dept. of Health and Human Services, Bethesda, MD; 94, courtesy of Planned Parenthood Foundation of America, NY.

Illustrations: page 5, copyright 1990 by Dorothy Carter; pages 69, 77, and 88 copyright 1991 by Michael Bryant.

The publisher also wishes to thank Mari Evans for permission to reprint her poem, *I Am A Black Woman* on the frontispiece of this collection.

Cover Design: Cheryl Willis Hudson

INDEX